**PRINT CASEBOOKS 3/THIRD ANNUAL EDITION
THE BEST IN ANNUAL REPORTS**

Conceived by
Martin Fox

Text and Introduction by
Rose M. DeNeve

Published by
**RC Publications, Inc.
Washington, D.C.**

INTRODUCTION

Copyright © 1978 by RC Publications, Inc. All rights reserved.

Published by RC Publications, Inc.
6400 Goldsboro Road NW
Washington, D.C. 20034

No part of this publication may be reproduced or used in any form or by any means—graphic, electronic, or mechanical, including photocopying, recording, taping, or information storage and retrieval systems—without written permission of the publisher.

Manufactured in U.S.A.
First Printing 1978

PRINT CASEBOOKS 3/THIRD ANNUAL EDITION/THE BEST IN ANNUAL REPORTS
Library of Congress Catalog Card Number 75-649581
ISBN 0-915734-20-6

PRINT CASEBOOKS 3/THIRD ANNUAL EDITION
Complete 6-Volume Set
ISBN 0-915734-18-4

RC PUBLICATIONS
President and Publisher: Robert Cadel
Vice President and Editor: Martin Fox
Art Director/Designer: Andrew P. Kner
Associate Editor: Teresa Reese
Associate Art Director: Rose M. DeNeve
Business Manager: Howard Cadel
Editorial Consultant: David R. Brown
Title Page Illustration: Isadore Seltzer

Designing an annual report is no simple task. Perhaps more than any other printed piece produced by a corporation, the annual report must amplify all that is right with a company —its products, its people, its performance. For it is the annual report that speaks to actual and potential shareholders, who, after all, are the "owners" of these companies that are the "engines" of our economic system.

But an annual report is first and foremost a legal document, stemming as it does from Security and Exchange Commission rulings pertaining to disclosure of income and outgo of publicly-held businesses. Such disclosure becomes the point of scrutiny for investors and their agents, the brokers and analysts, and it stands to reason that a company whose disclosure— whose annual report—is more appealing in an economic (and perhaps esthetic, although this point is open to debate) sense will attract more buyers for its stock.

While there is some question as to just how important a role the design of an annual report plays in attracting investors, today's business community recognizes the potential of the annual report as a public relations tool. A designer can help a company with a bad year look better, can stimulate interest in a company far beyond the tallies on its balance sheets, can humanize highly technological products and visualize intangible services. Through design, an annual report can even create an identity for a company that is new and unknown or for an older one that has gone through a change in management policy.

"Identity" is an elusive quality. One designer defines it as "the sum of all of the communications produced by a company for its employees, its customers and its publics"—the impression left and the feeling generated by the visual realization of the verbal mode. And this is where the designer fits in, for the designer is the molder of the visual realization and, hence, indirectly of a company's identity.

In designing that paradigm of corporate identity, the annual report, the designer must, as David Brown noted in the introduction to an earlier Annual Report Casebook, enter into a business relationship containing "appropriate amounts of cash and compromise." There is not the freedom to inject a considerable amount of ego, as in, say, designing a poster or even a capabilities brochure. Corporate management watches the development of its annual report very carefully, looking for a report that is at once attractive and innovative in terms of design, yet stalwart and conservative in terms of its being a business communications piece. Thus, corporations are hesitant to incorporate into their annual reports anything which hasn't been done before.

This unwillingness to experiment with the annual report as a form has resulted in a leveling off of the upward trend that has been observed in annual report design since the 1960s. As one Casebook juror observed, "We had an upgrading of the masses in terms of design, but the trend has flattened, so that instead of design getting continually better, more and more of it looks the same."

Some corporations virtually do turn out the same report year after year—they have adopted a standardized scheme and each year insert new photos and figures into essentially the same frames. Interestingly, some of these reports appeared in past Casebooks, but, despite their continuing and still handsome formats, were not, with one or two exceptions, selected for this Casebook. One explanation for this is that Casebook juries change from year to year, and what appeals to one panel does not necessarily appeal to another. But another reason is that, in some instances, the reports themselves simply no longer looked special enough to command interest.

It is also interesting to note why some good-looking reports were rejected out-of-hand. In many cases, an otherwise beautifully produced report was dismissed because of a conventionally designed cover. (The jurors were careful to select reports which they felt succeeded on all levels of design and worked as a complete unit.) Some reports were simply too laden with clichés—photo themes including burly roughnecks, Tall Ships, oil rigs in the sunset, or Bicentennial celebrations were likely candidates for the reject pile. (Incidentally, the reject pile was also the place for those reports with signatures missing or misbound, or with blank pages inside—regardless of their merits. It would behoove future Casebook competition entrants to check that their reports are perfect samples before submitting them.)

The fact is that most entries submitted for this Casebook— and even some of the winners —were formula-followers, using photographs, preferably large (in four-color or in black-and-white duotone), a Helvetica typeface (alone or in combination with another face), conventional-looking charts (usually the vertical bar variety). Those winning reports which did take chances in terms of design were either for large, highly successful corporations who are dominant in their industries and hence have the confidence to risk visual experimentation, or for newer, smaller companies anxious to portray themselves as innovators.

Of these smaller company reports, many of which were from the West Coast, Casebook juror Mike Schacht observed, "These reports have a handcrafted-on-the-West-Coast look. Fewer reports are produced out there, so there's not as much pressure on printers as there is in the East." To which juror John Morning added, "A new company doing a small run will use a small printer and perhaps get better attention. With a large run at a large printing house, a job sometimes gets lost in the shuffle."

While the standard annual report "form" was not tampered with this year (there

5/Annual Reports

were no boxed reports, or newspaper-style reports, and only a few folder-type or multiple-booklet reports), there was some manipulation of details which, taken together, might be seen as minor trends in annual report design.

Perhaps the most common deviation from the norm noted during the judging was what came to be called "the mysterious photograph." Photography is an annual report mainstay, but several reports featured abstract shots of complicated technical products, or dramatically lit close-ups of more sculptured ones; often these photos were de-mystified with an accompanying diagram or full-product shot that explained the object and its use.

While charts have been a point of innovation in the past —in some reports, charts have been the sole graphic motif— this year saw little beyond pies, bars, and upward-stepping lines. One report, however—for Heinz—sliced a luscious, ripe tomato with hairline rules to indicate capital expenditures; others, notably the St. Regis report, combined simpler charts with text in an unusual way.

One area of innovation appearing this year—the dramatic scaling and placement of folios—suggests that annual report designers really are reaching for ways to enliven the humdrum formula. In a few reports, the folios were sculptured forms, or scaled up to 60 picas and prominently placed at the top or side of the page. As one juror mused during the judging, is a folio worth this attention? (For a discussion of artifice vs. appropriateness, see the introduction to the second Annual Report Casebook.)

Production techniques, too, saw little innovation beyond halfsheets and foldouts, diecuts and embossing, and even these were not much in evidence. One report, however, was rejected for its excesses in this area. In what appeared to be an imitation of the Wall Street Journal, the report was designed in standard 8½" by 11" format to feel like a newspaper, with lots of rules and serif type. The point of excess was reached with the decision to print the report on glossy stock, with a four-color rendition of newspaper stock printed as a background, complete with speckles, hairs and flecks.

But opulent printing has in itself become the norm. "Black-and-white" is no longer a simple one-color job, but a duotone of black and gray or brown, often with a varnish over the photographs. It is not unusual to find reports with nine-color runs—four-color process plus a couple of match colors for charts or rules, and two varnishes for elegant effects.

Last but not least, there is the area of theme. Most of the reports in this Casebook were designed around a two-track system: a straight track for text —the operations review—and a "theme" track for photos and captions—a company's prime identity-builder in terms of an annual report. The photo theme is generally related to company operations through people or products or both. Occasionally, however, the relationship of the visual theme to the corporate business is tenuous or even far-fetched, and such reports are not likely to be accepted into the ranks of Casebook winners.

But to one who, from a position outside the business and financial community, reviews hundreds of annual reports each year, the choice of themes even among some of the selected reports can be puzzling. Presumably, a theme is chosen with full consciousness of the audience to which the report is being presented—primarily, financial analysts and investors. Why, then, do some companies feel the need to go beyond a straightforward "who we are/what we do" approach to assume an almost defensive posture in explaining their dealings?

In responding to the questionnaire that is sent to all Casebook winners, one designer noted that his theme —showing employees on and off the job—"was conceived to counteract criticism of corporations as implacable, non-personal entities." Criticism from whom? Certainly not from the report's primary audience. Even the public-at-large recognizes that corporations are made up of people who are taxpayers and consumers like everyone else.

But the defensiveness runs deeper than that. One report, for Lomas & Nettleton mortgage investors, combines a straightforward text on the company's services—financing land development—with sensitive American Indian poetry and elegant, dramatic photographs that might have been produced by the Sierra Club. Are we really to believe that Lomas & Nettleton is also in the business of wilderness preservation? If it is, why doesn't the text say so, with full disclosure of land management policies of L & N mortgagees?

The annual report has also become a forum for voicing opinions on matters larger than the company's products or services. Several of this year's entries produced ringing defenses of the capitalist system, decrying government regulation and pleading for the return of unfettered free enterprise. Do shareholders who, by very investment of capital, have demonstrated their commitment to the American economic system, need to be given this kind of pep-talk? Why all this preaching to the converted?

—Rose DeNeve

Annual Reports/6

CASEBOOK JURORS

Don Shanosky

Don Shanosky is designer and principal in the firm of Cook & Shanosky Associates, a Princeton, NJ-based firm that has received national and international recognition in major design publications and exhibitions. Cook & Shanosky provides a wide variety of communication services for major corporations, institutions, foundations and government agencies. Shanosky's prior experience includes corporate design positions and independent consulting.

John Morning

Educated at Wayne State University in Detroit and New York's Pratt Institute, John Morning was an art director at McCann-Erickson before establishing his own firm, John Morning Design, Inc., in 1960. He was an instructor in graphic design at Pratt Institute during 1968-70 and is a member of Pratt's board of trustees. He also has been a member of the Museum of Modern Art Junior Council and on the board of directors of the Publishing Center for Cultural Resources.

Michael Schacht

Michael Schacht is vice president of Sanders Printing, New York City. He is active in the American Institute of Graphic Arts and the Printing Industries of Metropolitan New York. His designs have won numerous awards and several have sold nationally.

Andrew Kner

Born in Hungary in 1935, Kner is a member of the ninth generation of his family to be involved in design. He came to the U.S. in 1940, received his BA at Yale in 1957 and MFA in 1959. He has been art director of the promotion department of the New York Times since 1970, after a year as art director of the Times' Sunday Book Review. Before that he worked in promotion design for Esquire and Look magazines. He also has been art director of PRINT magazine since 1962, and graphics consultant to the National Endowment for the Arts since 1974.

Richard Rogers

Richard Rogers was senior designer with the Lester Beall design group and then manager of display, exhibition and graphic design with IBM before forming his own firm in New York City in 1969. His experience covers a wide variety of graphic projects, including trademarks, annual reports, sales promotion literature, publication styling, displays, exhibitions, packaging and audio-visual presentations. He received a Bruce Rogers memorial scholarship from AIGA while an undergraduate at the University of Illinois, where he graduated summa cum laude.

7/Annual Reports

CASEBOOK WRITER

Rose M. DeNeve

Since receiving her BA in design in 1969 from Harpur College, State University of New York at Binghamton, Rose DeNeve has been employed by RC Publications, where she is now managing editor of PRINT magazine. She has written numerous articles on people and events in the design community, and has also reviewed books on photography and the applied arts for Harper's Bookletter and Americana magazine. DeNeve is also a freelance designer, and has designed covers, catalogs, brochures and other promotional material for a variety of clients.

INDEX Companies

Alza Corp. **18**
Amdahl Corp. **84**
American Telecommunications Corp. **25**
Bradford National Corp. **49**
Champion International Corp. **64**
Colt Industries, Inc. **94**
Cummins Engine Co. **39**
First Boston, Inc. **46**
Great Northern Nekoosa Corp. **42**
Heinz, H. J., Co. **21**
Hong Kong and Shanghai Banking Corp., The **35**
Lomas & Nettleton Mortgage Investors **80**
Manufacturers Hanover Corp. **57**
Mattel, Inc. **87**
Northrop Corp. **60**
Owens-Illinois **73**
Potlatch Corp. **90**
St. Regis Paper Co. **70**
Seagram Co. Ltd., The **13**
Smith International, Inc. **54**
Spencer Foundation, The **52**
Standard Brands Paint Co. **67**
Sweco, Inc. **28**
United California Bank **76**
Wallace Murray Corp. **16**
Warner Communications, Inc. **32**
West Chemical Products, Inc. **10**

Design Firms/Designers/Art Directors

Advertising Designers **28**
Bender, Lawrence **84**
Bender, Lawrence, & Associates **84**
Blackburn, Bruce **46, 73, 90**
Briggs, Al **18**
Charysyn, Taris **16**
Cleveland, John **25**
Cleveland, John, Inc. **25**
Cohen, Michael **25**
Cook, Roger **70**
Cook & Shanosky **70**
Corporate Graphics, Inc. **21**
Cross, James **54, 60, 76, 87**
Cross, James, Design Office **54, 60, 76, 87**
Danne, Richard **46, 90**
Danne & Blackburn **46, 73, 90**
Glassman, Bob **49**
Graphic Communication Ltd. **35**
Graphic Expression, The **49**
Harrison Associates **57**
Hess, Richard **64**
Hess, Richard, Inc. **64**
Hinrichs, Kit **32**
Hinrichs, Linda **32**
Hughes, Edward **52**
Hughes, Edward, Design **52**
Jonson Pedersen Hinrichs **32**
Marrin, James **28**
Matsubayashi, Chikako **67**
Morava, Emmett **76, 87**
Ohmer, Tom **28**
Olsen, Dagfinn **49**
Perman, Norman **42**
Perman, Norman, Inc. **42**
Rand, Paul **39**
Rice, Dick **18**
Richards, Stan **80**
Richards Group, The **80**
Robinson, Bennett **21**
Runyan & Rice **18**
Saks, Arnold **13, 16, 94**
Saks, Arnold, Inc. **13, 16, 94**
Scharrenbroich, Ingo **13, 94**
Schneider, Elliott **10**
Schneider Graphics **10**
Shanosky, Don **70**
Steiner, Henry **35**
Sullivan, Ron **80**
Tani, Dennis **25**
Tribich, Jay **57**
Wallin, Mark **84**
Weller, Don **67**
Weller Institute for the Cure of Design, The **67**

Photographers/Illustrators

Arrighi, Nike **35**
Barnett, Peggy **13**
Barnett, Ronald **13**
Beck, Arthur **70**
Beverly, Ike **39**
Booth, Greg **80**
Bullaty, Sonja **64**
Caplan, Stan **67**
Chia-lun, King **35**
Davidson, Bruce **21**
Erwitt, Elliott **46**
Farrell, Bill **49**
Fong, John **73**
Francisco & Booth **80**
Fusco, Paul **32**
Giusti, Robert **35**
Glinn, Burt **16**
Grehan, Farrell **13**
Hailey, Jayson **54**
Haling, George **64**
Hollyman, Tom **64**
Holmes, Nigel **35**
Huffman, Edwin **46**
ICOM, Inc. **73**
Kalisher, Simpson **64**
Lam, David **35**
Langley, David **64**
Liebowitz, Annie **32**
Loeb, Catherine **35**
Lomeo, Angelo **64**
Manham, Alan **35**
Marco, Phil **46**
McMahon, Franklin **42**
Meek, Richard A. **39**
Meinzinger, George **25**
Meyerowitz, Joel **16**
Nelson, Steve **18**
Newman, Arnold **57**
Olson, John **32**
Pugh, Anna **35**
Rossum, Cheryl **73**
Sasaki, Shoko **35**
Schneebli, Heini **73**
Shapero, Don **84**
Sherrod, David **28**
Silver, Marv **18**
Slobodian, Scott **76, 87**
Soned, Leonard **10**
Stage, John Lewis **64**
Sze-Keung, Liu **35**
Tachibana, Kenji **28**
Tatsumi, Shiro **35**
Turner, John Terrence **39**
Uzzle, Burk **16, 90, 94**
Volquartz, Per **60**
Weller, Don **67**
Whitmore, Ken **25**
Wolf, Werner **64**
Yamao, Akio **35**

9/Annual Reports

West Chemical Products

In reviewing this year's crop of winners in the Annual Report Casebook, it is interesting to note that there are a substantial number of smaller companies who seek out top-flight report design.

Such a company is West Chemical Products, a $75-million-in-sales corporation specializing in chemicals and pharmaceuticals "serving the needs of environmental sanitation and human and animal health." Its 1976 annual report is a nice amalgam of fine printing, premium paper, and good design.

Aside from the operations review and financial disclosures basic to any annual report, there were two major areas of concern to both designer and client in developing this report. One was to depict West Chemical's three major areas of production; the other was to represent those areas as they are perceived by the user.

Designer Elliot Schneider prepared two design alternatives in keeping with the 20-page, two-color parameters of the assignment; after conferences with the client, a solution was adopted that used photography as the primary means of meeting both challenges of concern.

In addition, a structure was devised for separating the various divisions by means of stepped-back pages; each farther-projecting page is keyed with a symbol that indicates the product area, much as an index tab locates a specific point of reference. The symbols are graphic portrayals of a factory (environmental health), a human head

Annual Reports/10

(human health), and a cow (animal health), each dropped out in white from a medium gray cross that subliminally reinforces the health idea.

The photo essay attempts to use real people (as opposed to professional models) in conjunction with West products. So the cover presents a train conductor who "takes great pride in his job and in passenger comfort," and who is pleased to have a workman in the background using a West Chemical product to clean the train. A basketball player knows the importance of a smooth, clean gym floor; a nurse values medicines and solutions used in the operating room; a dairy farmer places emphasis on herd health as well as sanitary milk production methods. All of these portraits project a believable personality, and in each there is a West Chemical product—it may be slightly out of focus in the background, but we know it's there, and somehow we're glad.

Each photo is run in fine duotone black-and-white on the right-hand page of the spread; photos bleed top and bottom and butt the white "tab-indicator" band projecting along the right-hand edge. The left-hand page bears a single column of operations review text, set flush-left/ragged-right in a readable serif face.

A broad column of white space separates this text from the gutter column, where a brief caption explains the picture opposite and the items shown below—a vignetted halftone of the products manufactured by that

Chemicals for environmental sanitation and human and animal health are personalized through portraits of some of their beneficiaries; stepped-back pages with identifying symbols efficiently guide the reader to the business review for each of the company's three major product areas.

11/Annual Reports

particular division. A three-sided hairline box holds the caption and products against the gutter, thus unifying the pictorial material within the spread. Here and there, a shadow from one of the bottles or cartons slips beneath the hairline into the center white space, adding the feeling of a third dimension.

The financial section begins on page 10 with a full page printed in the medium gray used for the tab symbols. This color is also used to line front and back covers, and appears in the facilities-location map on the last page. This map, by the way, is another good bit of design, composed as it is from vertical rules printed alternately in the colors of the duotone.

Taken together, this report emits a humanness. The portraits—whose art direction, the designer writes, was one of the most satisfying aspects of this assignment—are framed with a sensitive hand, and we get the feeling of *real* people, *really* caring. The products, while dutifully represented, are not glorified but put into the context of use (neither glamour nor monument here). An ingenious structure involves the reader instantly with graphic symbols that invite opening at the various tabs (no flipping through pages to find out about one manufacturing division).

This is the first report designed by Schneider for West Chemical Products. Up to that point, no one had established a definite identity for this client. Schneider has used the annual report form to create and reinforce an identity, and has done it surpassingly.

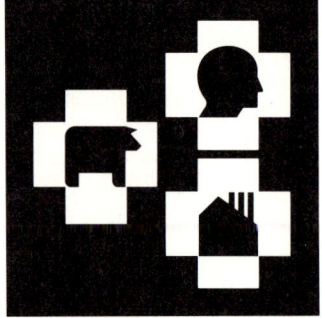

Report: West Chemical Products, Inc. 1976. Chemicals and pharmaceuticals for sanitation and health. 1976 sales $75 million.
Design firm: Schneider Graphics, New York
Art director/designer: Elliott Schneider
Photographer: Leonard Soned
Copywriter: George Auerbach
Printer: Sanders Printing
Size: 8½" by 11"; 20 pages plus covers
Quantity: 9000

● Branch Offices
■ Manufacturing Facilities
▲ Regional Distribution Centers
○ Corporate Offices

Annual Reports/12

Seagram

Seagram's 1975 annual report made a case for the company's bold leap from the wine and spirits business to the gas and oil industry. The '76 report sticks more closely to the market for which the company is best known and in which it has claimed the title of the world's largest producer and marketer of wines and distilled spirits.

As in other years, the opening portion of the report proper is the letter to shareholders, which for Seagram has been the place for an extensive operations review. Unlike the letters in some annual reports, this one puts aside any discussion of philosophy for the straight reporting of the facts: for the first time, Seagram sales passed the $2-billion mark; net earnings were $80.5 million.

The letter continues for eight pages on an ivory-colored Tweedweave stock, reviewing the successes of each of the company's major brands in the U.S. and abroad and reporting on its continuing commitment to oil and gas exploration. To the right of this running commentary, positioned by vertical hairline rules, is a series of black-and-white product vignettes with captions summarizing the facts put forth in the letter.

A Seagram report has appeared in each of the previous two Annual Report Casebooks, and one thing that made each of those winners special was the essay section that formed the heart of the non-regulated area of the report. The essay in the '74 report was about wine. In '75, it focused on oil. Here, the focus is on the liquor business

with a 20-page essay section on Seagram's "Commitment to Quality."

The section opens with a full-color bleed photograph of the company's head of quality control "nosing" a couple of samples of Seagram's best-selling V.O. The following pages are organized around a horizontal (much like the '75 report's oil essay) which places text above and photographs below for pages combining both; full-page photos are framed with just enough page-white to impart an elegant feel.

"Popular myth has it," the essay begins, "that with corporate growth must come a decline in caring, a gradual but relentless erosion of standards." Not so at Seagram, we are assured, where "history...demonstrates otherwise." The essay continues with a sensitive narrative in which a pioneer Seagram blender recalls his early days with the company working closely with founder Samuel Bronfman...a quality control coordinator for Seagram wines claims he is "not a poet of wine" but understands, feels and loves it...a senior blender speaks of guaranteeing the consumer the Seven Crown taste every time he buys it. It is a warmly human essay, concentrating as it does on both product quality and the experiences of those responsible for it and, like the previous report's essay on oil, the writing is several cuts above standard annual report fare.

In the center of this section there is a four-page "mini-essay"—printed on short sheets—spotlighting the

Quality products is the theme of this report, with a four-page mini-essay that was also used by Seagram as a mailer to a non-annual report audience.

Annual Reports/14

production of "the world's number one Canadian"—V.O. Here, the design format changes to a predominantly white page; essay text starts with an oversize cap and continues in 18-point Caledonia for the four pages. Vertical hairlines frame the single column of text and photos; the photos themselves—all in color—are like so many round-cornered snapshots pasted into an album. It's a nice device and, for Seagram's top brand, offers a quick-scan quality statement for those who can't or won't take the time to ponder the larger essay.

The financial pages of this report pretty much follow the rules laid down in previous years. They begin on a rag stock—this time in a rosy beige—with a list of contents and the heraldic Seagram seal; immediately following are the 15 bar charts seen in '75, updated, of course, for the '76 report. Again, vertical rules help to contain the figures here and in the balance sheets which follow.

Mention was made in the previous Casebook that the essay section on oil in the '75 Seagram report might have had a narrower appeal than one on wine or spirits. The essay here was plainly destined to reach a broad audience. Because Seagram felt it successfully presented the company's dedication to quality products, the designer tells us, the entire essay section was reprinted as a special mailing to a non-annual report audience.

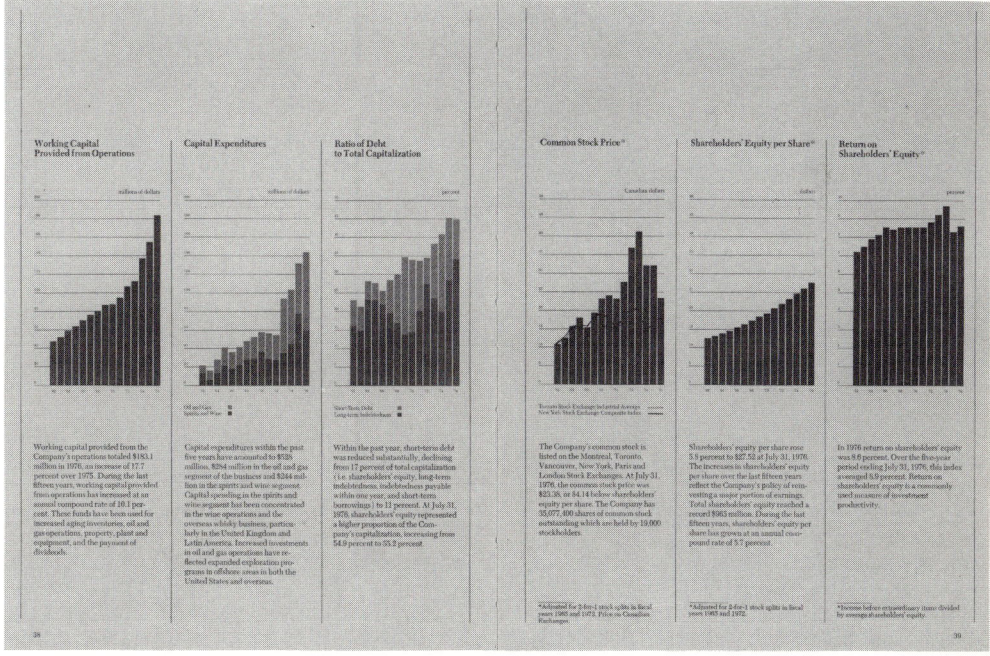

Report: The Seagram Company Ltd. 1976. Distilled spirits and wines; gas and oil exploration and production. 1976 sales $2 billion.
Design firm: Arnold Saks, Inc., New York
Art director: Arnold Saks
Designers: Ingo Scharrenbroich, Arnold Saks
Photographers: Farrell Grehan (color), Peggy and Ronald Barnett (black-and-white)
Copywriter: Adams & Rinehart (public relations counsel)
Printer: Case-Hoyt
Size: 9" by 11½"; 54 pages plus covers
Quantity: 50,000

15/Annual Reports

Wallace Murray

What can be said about an annual report whose design typifies the form to perfection?

Arnold Saks has designed nine annual reports for Wallace Murray—many of them award-winners—but feels that the 1976 report is "the most efficient-looking of all." Perhaps efficiency is the key word here, for not an agate is wasted, whether in space or form.

Wallace Murray is a corporation involved in the manufacture and sale of building products, power components and cutting tools—the kind of hardware that especially lends itself to those beautifully-framed industrial photographs, such as the one of a gleaming pattern formed by metal gears that appears on the report's cover. And it is the kind of business that lends itself to an efficient, "machined" treatment in terms of design.

Basic to the treatment is a text module that sweeps across the center of each spread (although it actually sits slightly above the middle of the page). Above the text is a three-point rule, defining a broad top margin which holds various heads. Above the head a hairline defines the upper limits of the "live" area.

Below the text block is another hairline; a third marks the bottom margin. The space in between is used variously for graphs—brightly colored rectangles with dropped-out vertical bars—or nearly-square full-color photographs of various points of manufacture. Working with the copy module are four-corner-bleed color photographs showing the workaday world at various

Annual Reports/16

Wallace Murray facilities—coils of raw steel being unloaded in Idaho, a ceramics worker in Mississippi, custom gear-welding in Illinois. The photographs bring color, drama, life to the restrained textual treatment; their random placement on left- or right-hand pages precludes monotony and minimizes interruption of the report's horizontal flow.

Halfway through the book, the operations review ends and, without fanfare, the financial review begins. Text and tables here fit into the familiar copy module, but extend clear to the bottom hairline instead of leaving space for photos or charts. While a few of these pages look a bit text-heavy because of this decision, others offer plenty of relief when text or tables end well above the bottom rule.

An added nice touch: Front and back covers are lined with a solid, silvery color that plays off the glint of the many metals cropping up in photos inside.

Arnold Saks, it might be said, has become somewhat of a legend in his own time. Although he is perhaps better known for the kind of report he annually executes for Seagram's distillers—a considerably more expensive, almost opulent proposition—it is precisely this kind of design, as seen in the Wallace Murray report, that has earned the designer his formidable reputation.

Report: Wallace Murray Corporation 1976. Manufacture and sale of building products, power components and cutting tools. 1976 sales $337 million.
Design firm: Arnold Saks, Inc.
Art director: Arnold Saks
Designers: Arnold Saks, Taris Charysyn
Photographer: Joel Meyerowitz, Burt Glinn/Magnum, Burk Uzzle/Magnum
Copywriter: Mark Strage
Printer: Sanders Printing
Size: 8½" by 11"; 32 pages plus covers
Quantity: 25,000

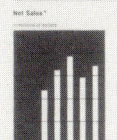
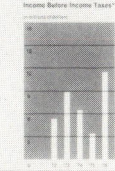

Full-color photographs and controlled use of type and rules spell efficiency for a manufacturer of machined tools and building products.

17/Annual Reports

Alza

Alza is a seven-year-old pharmaceutical research and development company that has never shown a profit. In fact, 1976, the year of this report, was the first in which Alza had any sales to report at all, and despite a $2.4-million net sales figure, the company still lost $17.8 million. And yet Alza's stock trades on the Pacific Exchange at respectable levels (27¼-14 were common-stock high and low for 1976).

The 1976 Alza annual report reveals in both content and style why this company is an attractive opportunity for investors: Alza is involved in precisely controlled drug delivery systems, an infant area of pharmaceutical research with a technological attraction—and promise— much like that of incipient new- and high-technology companies of the 1950s (Xerox being the prime example).

A review of the projects in which Alza is currently involved, as revealed in the pages of this report, seems akin to reading science fiction. The Ar/Med Infusor, for example, is a seven-ounce, portable intravenous apparatus that is worn by the patient to administer controlled doses of drugs directly into the circulatory system. Conventional administrative techniques, such as those for cancer chemotherapy, require a patient to be hospitalized and attached to a cumbersome overhead intravenous unit that requires him or her to remain nearly motionless during extended periods of treatment. The Ar/Med system allows the patient to pursue normal

Alza 1976 Annual Report

Annual Reports/18

physical activities during such treatment.

Similar exotic drug delivery systems include a nickel-sized patch that adheres to the skin and delivers scopolamine, a drug which combats motion sickness. Its advantages over oral applications during periods of "gastrointestinal distress" are obvious; moreover, since the system bypasses the liver, where scopolamine is metabolized, smaller doses of the drug can be used effectively. Alza sees this system as being applicable to other drugs, too.

There is also a "Minipump," an implantable research tool that can "deliver a continuous, precisely controlled flow of almost any biologically active agent into laboratory animals"; a contraceptive device inserted inside the uterus to administer small doses of progesterone over the course of a year (in a smaller yearly dose than the average woman produces in one day at the end of her menstrual cycle, and without the side effects of conventional oral contraceptives); a drug-administering device inserted weekly beneath the eyelids of patients with glaucoma. In addition to these and other drug-delivery projects, Alza research is involved with non-absorbable food additives and non-nutritive sweeteners.

This is the content of the Alza 1976 report—the promise of the future as not often seen in conventional company reports. Nor is the presentation of the future conventional in terms of report design.

"The production of this book dazzled me with its

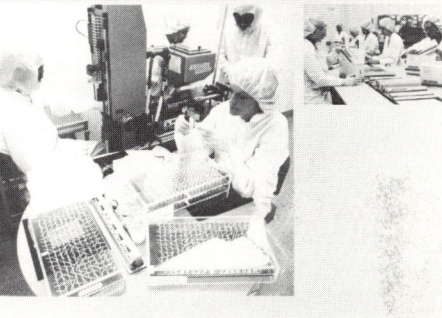

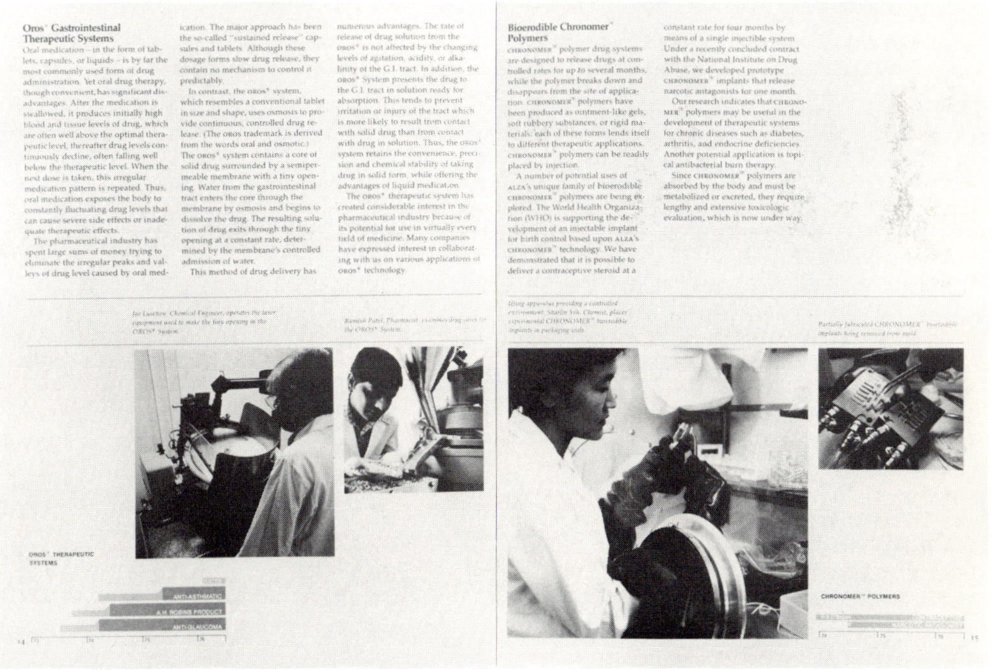

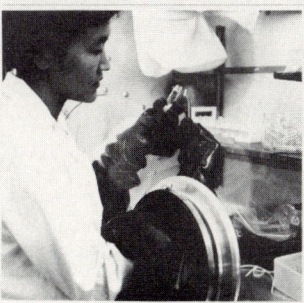

In this report, all four-color photos and charts are printed to butt a fifth color—a buffy glow for the background.

19/Annual Reports

footwork," commented Casebook juror Mike Schacht, although its richly embossed cover doesn't suggest the fancy printing inside. The book opens with the president's letter, which is followed by a product development chart spread across two pages. The chart is a beautiful piece of design, revealing the stages of development of Alza systems through time—from initial research through development, testing, regulatory review and marketing. Variously deepening earth colors indicate the length of time spent in each stage as a product is traced through its circuitous path. Impressing on the reader the enormous amount of time spent in meeting regulatory standards and gaining Federal Drug approval was an important concern in designing this report, and the ever-broadening lines of the chart reveal this process effectively.

This chart, as is the rest of the operations review section of this report, is printed on what appears to be a buff-colored stock. Actually, all four-color work—the chart and photographs—were printed to butt a fifth color used for the background. Even the "white" pages used for the financial review at the back of the book are not white but reveal a fine screen of this fifth color when put under a lens.

The design format itself is simple—text above, related photography below, with hairline rules holding captions in between. But it's that fancy footwork around the halftones that makes this report a winner.

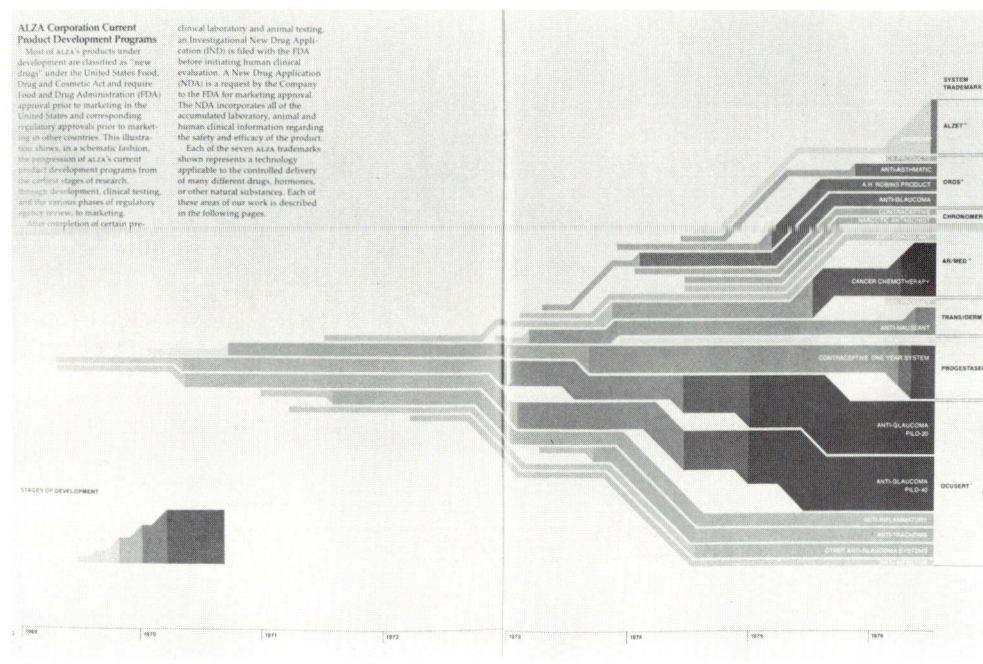

Report: Alza Corporation 1976. Creation, development and marketing of therapeutic delivery systems. 1976 sales $2.4 million.
Design firm: Runyan & Rice, Playa del Rey, CA
Art director: Dick Rice
Designer: Al Briggs
Photographers: Marv Silver, Steve Nelson
Copywriter: Saul Kent
Printer: George Rice & Sons
Size: 8½" by 11"; 32 pages plus covers
Quantity: 60,000

Annual Reports/20

H. J. Heinz

H. J. Heinz Company Annual Report 1977

Heinz is a company which, for no apparent reason, changes its annual report designer from year to year. And we can say for no apparent reason because the company's reports in general have always been superiorly designed—one has appeared in each of the three Annual Report Casebooks.

The Heinz annual reports for the years 1974 and 1975 focused on people—people using Heinz products in the former, people producing Heinz products in the latter. The 1977 report is also a people-watcher, but looks at Heinz employees as individuals rather than as they relate to their job with Heinz. A copy block on the report's cover states this theme succinctly enough: "Just as important to our fortunes are the people who work for us. A sampling, necessarily small, appears on these pages. Let them represent all those (and there are many more) who have found interesting and often novel ways to enrich their own lives and the lives of others." For those who miss the point on the cover, it is paraphrased inside in the letter to shareholders.

In the theme section, little is said of an employee's on-the-job performance other than to show a small photograph of the worker at his or her desk or in the plant and, next to it, set forth the person's name and title. The real focus of this report is what these people do in their off-the-job hours—from leading retarded boy scouts and caring for stray dogs to raising apples and breeding thoroughbreds or canaries. The theme was conceived, the designer tells

This year, we said, let's introduce some of the people who have helped to make Heinz so successful. We are, after all, a people-oriented company, sensitive to the specific demands of millions of persons around the world and tailoring our activities to their varying tastes.

Just as important to our fortunes are the people who work for us. A sampling, necessarily small, appears on these pages. Let them represent all those (and there are many more) who have found interesting and often novel ways to enrich their own lives and the lives of others.

We draw no conclusions. The stories speak for themselves. Just possibly, however, we may persuade some of our readers that no corporation should be thought of in impersonal terms. Rather, each corporation contains a host of very human individuals organized for common and useful purposes and enjoying the freedom to pursue outside activities of their own undictated choice.

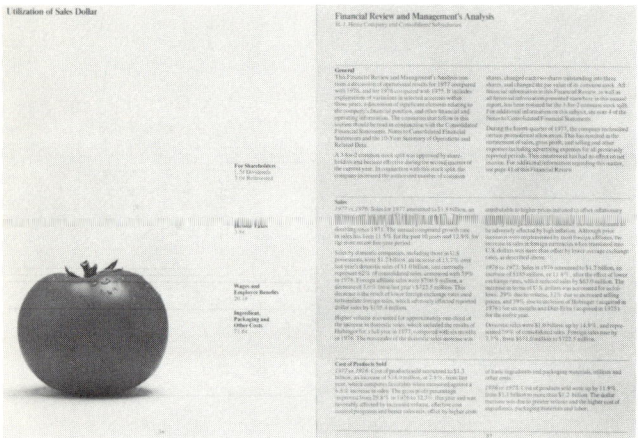

This report offers a glimpse into the private lives of various Heinz employees, thus presenting a corporation as a composite of caring individuals.

For Shareholders
1.5¢ Dividends
3.0¢ Reinvested

Income Taxes
3.8¢

Wages and Employee Benefits
20.1¢

Ingredient, Packaging and Other Costs
71.6¢

Annual Reports/22

us, "to counteract the criticism of corporations as implacable, non-personal entities." While we can't be sure who is doing the criticizing, the Casebook jurors felt that showing employees as decent, caring individuals was an effective solution. After all, what is a corporation if not the composite of all its employees?

Although all of the photographs are in black-and-white (a first for a Heinz report), they are given an added dimension through duotone printing which combines black with the gray-brown used for the text. In all, nine colors were used in printing this report, with various sections being variously printed.

There are a couple of other nice touches about this report —the most notable being the sheet that comprises pages 35 and 36. This is the one four-color sheet in the report, with the face bearing a group of six vertical bar charts colorfully depicting sales, income, earnings, expenditures, and return on equity and investment. The charts are separated from one another by hairline rules that will be recalled in the following financial section, and each is built up on a four-point rule that gives each stacking the effect of cans on a supermarket shelf.

The reverse of this sheet is a luscious, ripe tomato—what else could universally symbolize Heinz?—vignetted near the bottom of the page. Overprinted across it and stepping up to the right are hairline rules that indicate, with so many "slicings" of the tomato, where each Heinz

23/Annual Reports

sales dollar goes.

The financial review and management analysis that follows is a well-thought-out piece of design, with text and tables printed on a pale gray Linweave stock. Rather than being combined in a single, deadly text, each subject in the review is given its own two-column block, separated from the next by a rich blue hairline rule. The same blue is used to print the operating company tag that appears below the black headline at the top of the page.

Speaking of organization, it is worth noting the two instances of vertical halfsheets inserted in this perfect-bound report—one at the beginning to set forth table of contents, annual meeting notice, and company summary, and one to introduce the financial section at mid-report. This latter halfsheet also includes an index for the financial pages and notes about obtaining a copy of Heinz's 10-K form.

For those who have been checking off the previously mentioned nine colors, the remaining two will be found on the report's covers. The front cover is simply a block of text printed in the same brown used inside, with company and report identifier placed above a rule at the top. In the upper-left-hand corner is the well-known Heinz shield, printed in red. (This mark appears in red again on the back cover.) The ninth color is a tobacco brown used to line the covers. It is a warm complement to the tones of the text pages, and a unifying factor with the rest of the book.

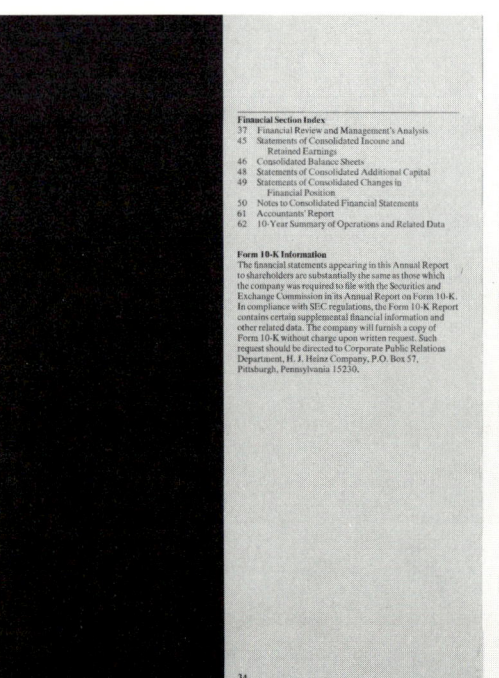

Annual Reports/24

Report: H. J. Heinz Company 1977. Food and food processing. 1977 sales $1.8 billion.
Design firm: Corporate Graphics, Inc., New York
Art director/designer: Bennett Robinson
Photographer: Bruce Davidson/Magnum
Copywriter: Oscar Scheffler
Printer: The Hennegan Co.
Size: 8½" by 11¼"; 66 pages plus covers
Quantity: 40,000

American Telecommunications

"Nineteen seventy-seven was a bad year for American Telecommunications!" forthrightly announces this report in its opening line. Despite a 23 percent increase in sales over 1976 figures, American Telecommunications lost money for the first time since its founding over a decade ago; its stock, which traded for as much as $9⅞ in the first quarter of 1977, was down as low as $3¾ by year-end.

The problem posed in putting together an annual report for a company coming out of a "bad year" is how to report the facts without destroying investor confidence. This report tries the direct approach, as indicated by the opening line, and fairly well succeeds.

Operations-review copy is written in first-person-plural, which gives it a warmth usually lacking in annual reports. The tone of the writing approaches the terse, to-the-point language used in some advertising, yet its openness makes the reader feel that the person talking—the president/chairman—has the situation under control ("Everything we did worked"). Despite a heavy write-off for backed-up inventory and other loss factors, the company was able to turn its finances around in the last quarter and, the president tells us, "we are infinitely stronger for the experience."

This turnaround, coupled with certain factors affecting the company's business, does indeed serve to instill confidence. Advances in telecommunications technology, government

25/Annual Reports

antitrust pressure aimed at telephone company-owned manufacturing subsidiaries, and increased demand for telecommunications products will set the stage for future growth, we are confidently assured. And American Telecommunications, with a new nuts-and-bolts philosophy of doing one thing supremely well—manufacturing telecommunications equipment —will put the firm in a position to reach "hard, no-nonsense, short-term, bottom-line performance."

The visual format for this annual report aptly enhances the warmth and personal appeal of the text. Rich black-and-white duotone photographs, each focusing on one aspect of American Telecommunications' business, are run across five consecutive spreads. The photos are varnished for added richness, and each is split by a halfsheet that opens to reveal—in the same clear language—the story of that division for the business year. All of the photographs include equipment manufactured by American Telecommunications as well as the people who manufacture it. Again, something personal. The halfsheet report pulls the reader into the photograph, and presents the text in a scale which is both intimate and inviting. (Interestingly, the photo spreads have no page numbers. Folios are assigned instead to the halfsheets, which makes total numbered pages add up to a curious 30.)

Charts in this report take the form of simple bar graphs, printed in medium gray at the end of each divisional report.

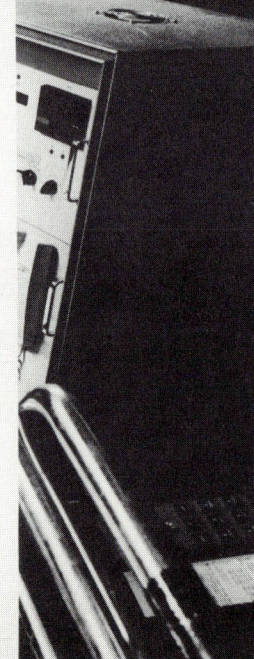

A bad year looks better in a report whose editorial matter is straight from the shoulder and whose visuals enhance the personal appeal of the text.

Annual Reports/26

In the financial review, however, we find a chart with a most unusual disclosure—the major factors contributing to the company's 1977 losses are spelled out in per-share figures. A similar chart compares the previous year with 1975. Again, this report is unusually aboveboard. In the same vein, a graph on the following page shows pointblank the firm's sources of invested capital.

So, here we have a report for a bad year. There is richness in the photography, candor in the writing, intimacy in the halfsheets, clarity in the charts, openness in the disclosures. The designer notes that, in making the decisions he did, he hoped to convey the feeling of "a strong, coordinated company working toward a single goal." His solution was obviously given much thought, for, to paraphrase the president's message, everything he did worked.

Report: American Telecommunications Corporation 1977. Telecommunications equipment. 1977 sales $26 million.
Design firm: John Cleveland, Inc., Los Angeles
Art director: John Cleveland
Designers: John Cleveland, Michael Cohen, Dennis Tani
Photographers: George Meinzinger, Ken Whitmore
Copywriter: American Telecommunications
Printer: Anderson Lithograph
Size: 8½" by 11"; 40 pages plus covers
Quantity: 15,000

27/Annual Reports

Sweco

This is a lot of annual report for a little company.

Sweco is a manufacturer of esoteric equipment for industry —the machinery, for example, which removes sand and other particulate matter from gas and oil well drillings while retaining valuable resources, or the mills that grind "a particle the size of a period (.) into more than 12 million smaller pieces." In 1976, the company's sales were just below $27 million, representing a 53 per cent improvement over 1975's figures.

The problem encountered by Advertising Designers in producing this report was to keep within the budget of the previous two-color report, and to keep it to the same number of pages. The report also had to be produced quickly— within two and a half months of initial client contact.

Advertising Designers has designed 20 annual reports for this client, a track record which undoubtedly eased the design and production process for this one. There is much to be gained from a long association with a client, not the least of which is a solid understanding of the company's goals and philosophy.

Although three ideas were presented to Sweco management for approval, two proved too involved in terms of research for the short production schedule. The solution adopted may have been "the least difficult on the part of the client" to produce, but it has all the attributes of a long-range-plan report.

One phenomenon commented on by Casebook jurors was the increasing use

of "mysterious photography" in annual reports—photos of product details or, perhaps, arcane products themselves that make for interesting and dramatic visuals but impart little information.

The photographs used in this report are details of arcane products whose intricate forms and repeating patterns offer visual relief with an interplay of light and shadow. But the reader is prepared for their mysteriousness by a statement which appears inside the report's front cover: "Some of the diverse textures, shapes and materials used in manufacturing Sweco products are captured in a dramatic series of photographs for this year's annual report." To this is added a brief note explaining each of the six pictures appearing on the cover or inside the report.

But the report goes further in unraveling its photographic mysteries by including next to each photo a line drawing of the object depicted, cut away and augmented with lines and arrows to indicate both the motion of the machine and the movement of processed materials through it. The red accent color used to line the report's covers and to pop out heads throughout the book is here employed to indicate motion and matter—a great help in reading these diagrams.

Beneath each diagram a short caption block explains the product and its purpose; the remainder of that column is blank, providing some white space against the uneven columns of text that complete the spread.

Photographs are all

To Our Shareholders

2

1976 was an outstanding year for SWECO. Both earnings and sales reached record levels. The corporation and its subsidiaries posted net profits of $1,135,000 ($17.73 per share), a 53% improvement over 1975's total of $743,000 ($11.60 per share) as restated. 1976 sales of $26,714,000 were 17% greater than the $22,847,000 recorded in 1975. Dividends paid to stockholders in 1976 were $2.40 per share versus $2.20 per share in 1975 — the sixth consecutive year of increased payout.

We are very pleased with the Company's overall growth, especially in view of a number of obstacles faced during the year. A costly four week labor stoppage with resultant production delays, the addition of new manufacturing facilities, a short-term drop in oil drilling activity, and the failure of the capital goods industry to maintain a growth rate at least equal to the Gross National Product were a few of the challenges that confronted the Company. Also international currency fluctuations created significant losses during the year.

SWECO is reporting gains or losses in translation of foreign currencies in compliance with the Financial Accounting Standards Board Ruling No. 8. This accounting change resulted in a charge against 1976 income of $101,000 or $1.58 per share due to substantial fluctuations in the value of the Belgian franc, Spanish pesata and Mexican peso. Excluding losses from foreign currency translations, SWECO exceeded its corporate goal of 15% return on shareholders' equity by achieving a 17% return during the year. However, because of the translation losses, this ROE fell to 14.1%.

SWECO's capacity to respond successfully to these challenges and move ahead to new levels of sales and profit is significant. Of course, the modest upswing in the domestic economy played a part in our progress this year, as did the slowing rate of inflation and lower interest rates. Most importantly, however, people in the Company worked extremely hard in a well coordinated effort to achieve these results.

Financial Changes

During 1976, progress was made in strengthening the financial base of the Company. With the growth in sales, profit margins and more effective controls, SWECO generated funds sufficient to reduce debt, to supply working capital needs and to expand fixed assets by 19%. The Company's cash position and inventory turnover improved.

As noted in our 1976 second quarter report, and following the terms of our 1974 financing agreement with the Bank of America, outstanding short-term debt amounting to $1.9 million was converted to a five year term note on July 1, 1976. On the same date, the bank also extended a short term line of credit of $1.3 million to the U.S. Company and $1.5 million to our European subsidiary for the financing of working capital.

Last year, we reported that the Company's financial and operating information systems were being transferred from a time-sharing arrangement to a leased, in-house computer, the intermediate-size UNIVAC 90-30. The conversion to the new computer format was completed as planned by the end of 1976. These systems are now operational as is a new inventory control program also mentioned in prior reports. A Forecasting and Material Requirements Planning (MRP) program is nearly complete and is scheduled for start-up before midyear. These programs should have a positive impact on future earnings.

Innovation and Evolution

Many elements contribute to a company's ability to evolve in step with the accelerating pace of industrial technology. Of prime importance is a constantly updated set of clearly articulated goals defining what the corporation wants to achieve and the structure by which it will reach these goals. At SWECO, this process has developed through careful planning and continual experimentation built upon that invaluable commodity . . . experience. The objectives include a determined corporate commitment to long-range growth.

Numerous strategies compose the methodology by which this growth is to be attained. The first tenet is that the bulk of our new products will emanate from internal development as opposed to random corporate acquisitions. While this

3

10

1977 and Beyond

The present year has started with a significant increase in new orders. Though it is too early to view this as a twelve month trend, the Company is optimistic that this growth pattern can be sustained.

At its meeting on January 27th, the board of directors voted to increase the regular quarterly dividend to 75¢ payable on March 1, 1977 to stockholders of record on February 15, 1977.

At the same meeting, Kenneth F. Julin was elected to the board of directors. Mr. Julin is the former chairman of the board of the Leach Corporation and past president of Custom Component Switches Company. His extensive knowledge of mechanical and electrical engineering as well as his general business experience will contribute importantly to the future strength and growth of the Company.

We would like to take this opportunity to express our deep appreciation to SWECO's management, employees and sales representatives for their outstanding efforts. 1976 was an exceptional year, and the achievements of these individuals provide all of us with the inspiration to seek even greater levels of performance in the future.

Sincerely,

Robert P. Miller, Jr.
Chairman of the Board

Howard W. Wright, Jr.
President

March 31, 1977

11

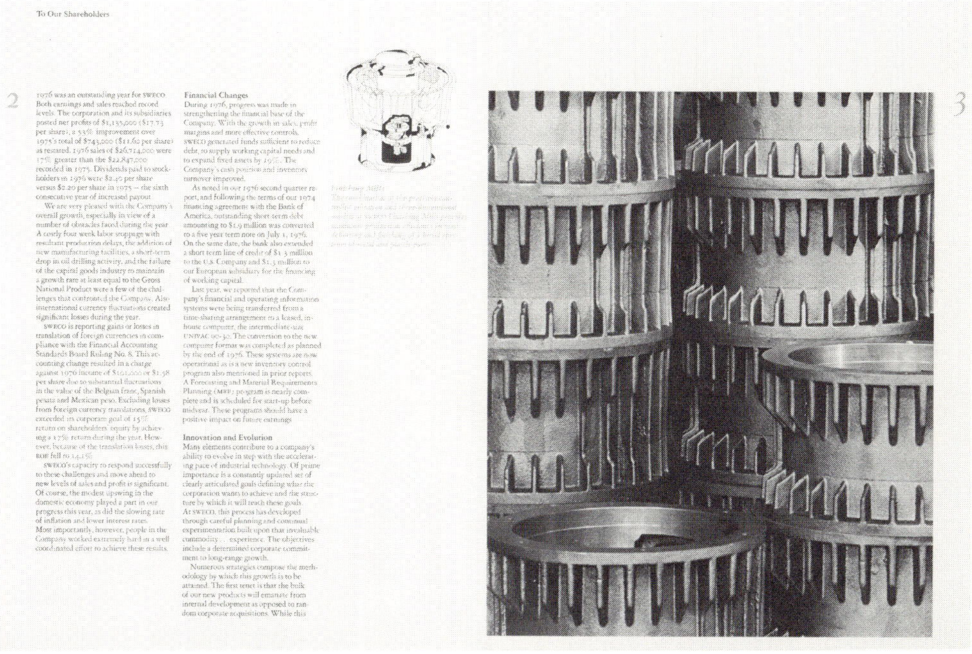

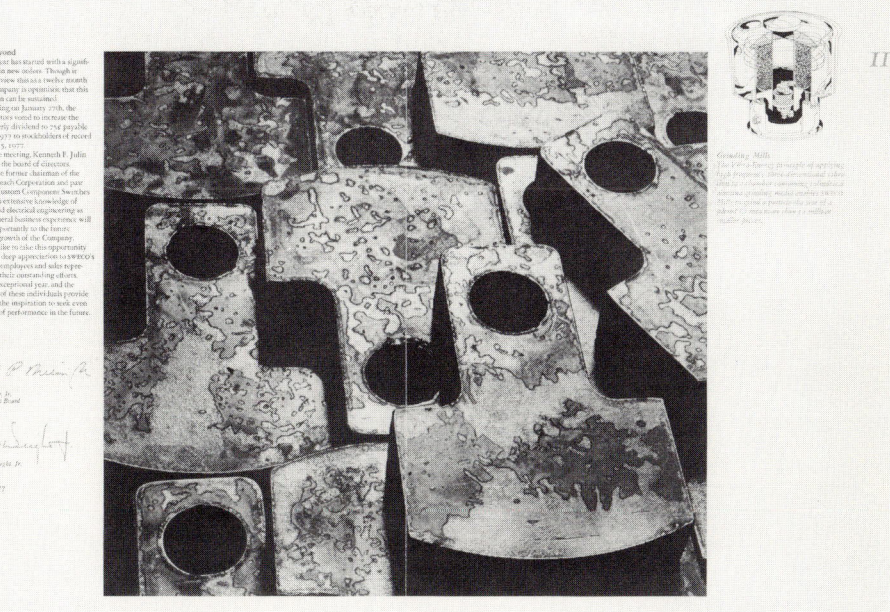

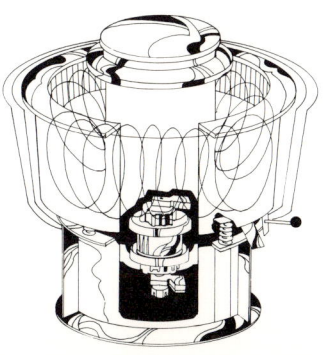

Close-up photographs of arcane products are demystified by diagrams of the complete products and what they do.

black-and-white, printed duotone on a Kromekote stock that needs no varnish to impart a feel of luxury. The designers were able to keep costs down by using the same stock (100-lb. text) for the report's covers, and by reducing the overall number of pages in the report.

There are a few other elements which add to the reserve and sophistication of this report. One is the handling of headlines, referred to earlier; although they are printed in red, they are merely scaled in a bolder version of the text-sized Garamond—no flashy face or outsize proportions. Another is the handling of charts and graphs. Tabular material is set simply; the same text face appears organized within hairline rules at the top of the designated page. The one real chart in the book, which breaks down a seven-year record of sales, income, earnings, assets and equity, is comprised of a year-by-year series of dots arranged horizontally across the page. The dots are printed in two colors—the accent red and the gray from the duotone —to indicate variously domestic and foreign sales, dividend and retained earnings, current assets and net property. Each record is separated from the others by a hairline rule.

The third element of luxury here is the generous proportion of white space. The uneven columns and airspace around the product diagrams has already been mentioned; in addition, the upper margin of the design format is a full ten picas from the trim-line; in the financial report, there may

Annual Reports/30

be nearly half a page left inviolate beneath a table.

An unusual treatment of folios completes the scheme—page numbers are set just below the top margin at the outside of each page, and are printed in gray in a 42-point Garamond Italic face.

As has been noted elsewhere in these pages, more and more small companies like Sweco are attaining a high level of annual report design. And if the number of them appearing in this Casebook is any indication, good design doesn't have to be priced out of the budget of the smaller corporation.

Report: Sweco, Inc. 1976. Separating, grinding and milling equipment for industry. 1976 sales $27 million.
Design firm: Advertising Designers, Los Angeles
Art director: Tom Ohmer
Designer: James Marrin
Photographer: Kenji Tachibana
Illustrator: David Sherrod
Copywriter: Cochrane Chase Advertising
Printer: Gardner/Fullmer Lithograph
Size: 8½" by 11"; 20 pages plus covers
Quantity: 5000

31/Annual Reports

Warner Communications

"This is a gaudy annual report for a gaudy business," remarked one Casebook juror in evaluating this annual report. Yet, the design of this report is not so much gaudy as it is contrived, much as is the entertainment business itself: This is a report that makes a show of "showtime."

The entire report is set in a spectrum of gray and black. Black covers bear naught but the gray-and-black Warner symbol, with the obligatory identifying copy dropped out in white. Inside pages are printed a flat warm gray; type is Stymie for text and Franklin Gothic for heads, printed in black and set off with thick black rules. The inside front cover is again black, with a financial highlight chart dropped out, as are a divisional listing and the table of contents. Here and there on text pages a headline or rule or bold, oversized cap drops out to spotlights of white. Now and then a marginal chart appears, with white bars dropping out of colored spots.

What all of this does is merely set the mood for the five pictorial sections of the book, one for each of Warner's divisions, much as a darkened theater focuses all attention on the lighted stage or screen.

The "entertainment" presented in the divisional picture sections is the heart of Warner Communications' business, and the heart of this report. The various sections of the report are formed by solid black pages, with text and financial highlights—a bit of good financial reporting—dropped out from the opening left-hand page. The photos are featured on a series of short sheets, and all are full-color, high-contrast shots of Warner entertainment.

In the "Recorded Music & Music Publishing" section, for example, there is a montage of Warner album covers covering a full picture spread; other pages show shots of recording artists or a crowd at a Beach Boys concert. A running text that starts on the opening full page is picked up again on the closing right, with short paragraphs describing the business year for each segment within Warner's music division.

When that last, full right-hand page is turned, another curtain goes up—this time it's "Motion Pictures and Television," with the photo "insert" showing Warner visual entertainment around the world.

The following last three acts are fairly short scenes from publishing, electronic games development and marketing, and cable communications. Each short-sheet section is organized within its own full-sheet wrapper.

For each section, a chart spells out sources of revenues and pre-tax income. Type has been organized to fall within the depth of the short sheets; thus, when the pictorials are flipped altogether left or right, a neat black border is formed by the projecting black "wrapper." In this space the designer has organized thumbnail color photographs and bold-faced summaries of the operations review. Like brief reviews on the TV and movie pages of a local newspaper—or perhaps the blurbs on an album cover or

Like a lighted stage or screen in a darkened theater, this report's full-color photography pops out of a black background: it's showtime. What better way to present a company whose business is entertainment?

book jacket—these notes capitalize on the entertainment theme.

The financial pages number 20 in this 72-page report, not counting the four at the front of the book which detail income, outgo, amortization and return on investment. Again, Stymie text, black rules and white, spotlighted-headlines appear on a medium-gray printed background. Whenever 1976 figures are compared with a previous year (or years), those figures are spotlighted by being dropped out in white; totals in each listing are further separated out by one- and two-point white rules. While this doesn't necessarily make the financial information easier to read, it does make quite a show of what often is tediously presented printed matter.

Art director/designer Kit Hinrichs notes that, in designing this report, more stock movie photographs had to be used than were originally planned or desired; yet "the realism required to accurately describe the company this year dictated the use of photographs." Dividing the pictorials into their own special sections proved the best method of organization for both visuals and editorial matter.

"We were trying to project graphically," Hinrich adds, "what in reality Warner Communications is—an intelligent, creative, aggressive, profitable, highly complex organization that understands itself and the environment in which it operates."

Hinrichs also notes that production of this complicated book demanded the ingenuity

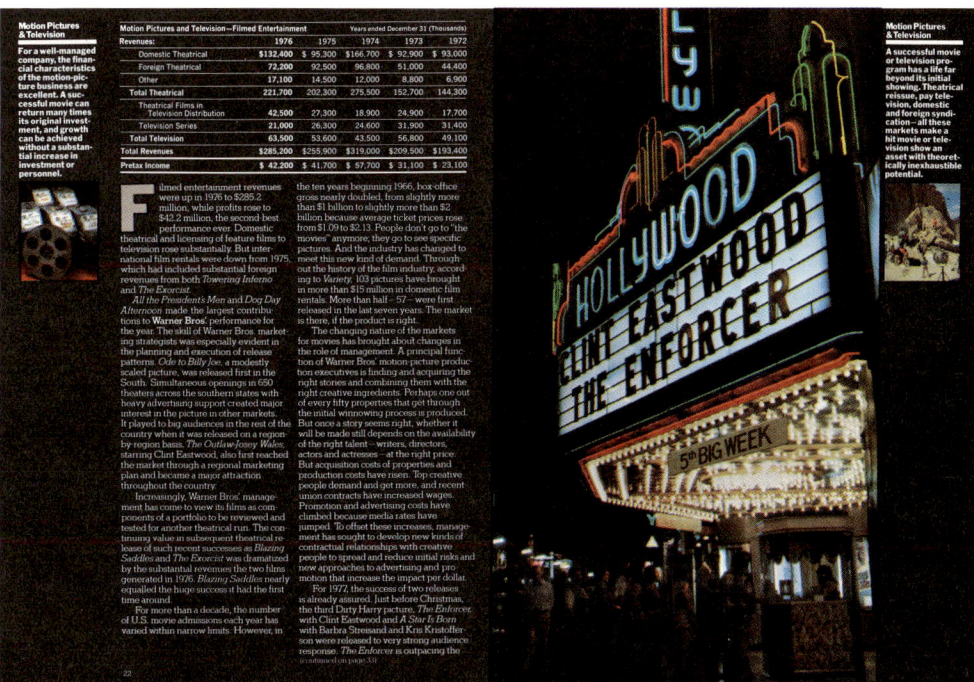

33/Annual Reports

of the printer to overcome certain obstacles. "The job was originally planned to run in eight colors—four-color process, matte black, matte gray and two varnishes—in one five-color pass and one three-color pass, with numerous 'trapped' photos. This created two problems, the first being the need for 100-lb. coated text for tight registration —and the accompanying increase in paper and postage costs as well as an undesirable bulk in the report. The second problem was the difficulty of checking and correcting the black or gray photo backgrounds while the report was on press."

The printer suggested shooting the process-black printer very sharp so that matte-black ink could be substituted for process ink, enabling both black areas to be printed in one pass— thereby eliminating one "color" from the last press pass. This complex production formula—and its unqualified success—proved for Hinrichs to be the most satisfying aspect of designing the Warner Communications 1976 report.

Report: Warner Communications, Inc. 1976. Music recording, motion picture, television and electronic entertainments. 1976 revenues $826.8 million.
Design firm: Jonson Pedersen Hinrichs, San Francisco
Art director: Kit Hinrichs,
Designers: Kit Hinrichs, Linda Hinrichs
Photographers: John Olson, Paul Fusco, Annie Liebowitz
Copywriter: Warner Communications
Printer: Case-Hoyt
Size: 9" by 12"; 72 pages plus covers
Quantity: 70,000

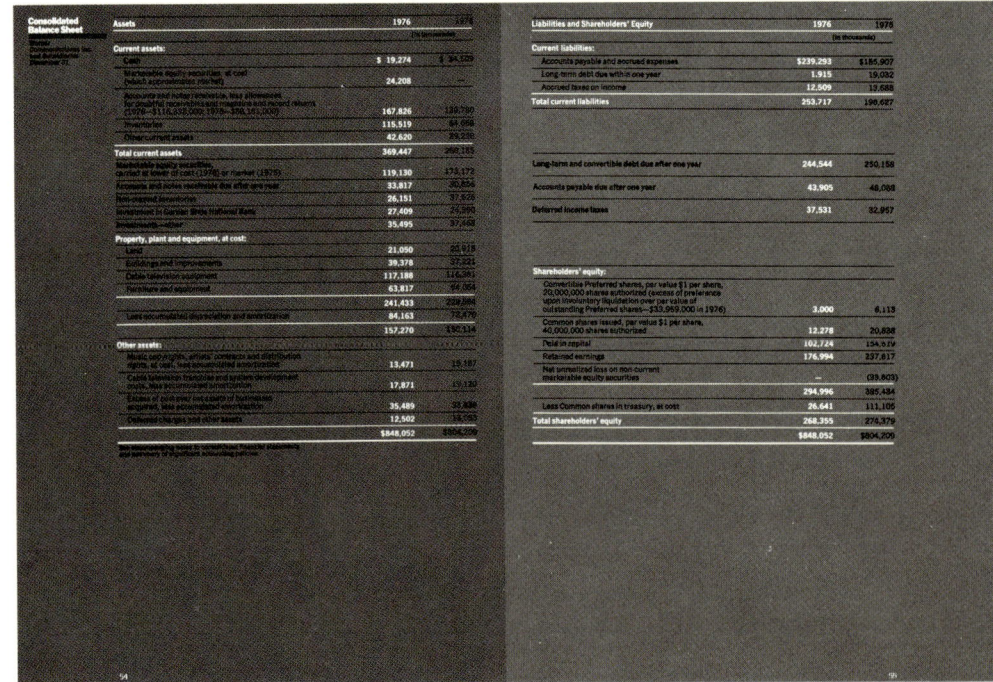

Annual Reports/34

Hongkong and Shanghai Banking

Henry Steiner has been designing the annual report for the Hongkong and Shanghai Banking Corporation for ten years, and one has appeared in each of the three Annual Report Casebooks.

This bank's stock is not traded publicly in the U.S., so the kind of information contained in this report is a bit different from that issued by SEC-regulated corporations. However, the basic annual report design problem remains the same. There is certain copy which must be worked into a visual theme, and certain financial information which must be presented carefully and attractively.

For the past eight years, the reports for this bank have been built around strong visual themes, such as handicrafts, tourism, education, housing, transportation, and the like. The '76 report's theme is "Environment," hence the big "E" on the cover. And unlike the reports published by the bank since 1971—all of which were three volumes held in a pocketed folder—this report is bound into a single volume.

To give the feeling of separate entities, however, the financials have been presented first as straight tabular material printed in black and brown on buff-colored rag stock. In this section, too, are the chairman's statement and the lists of board members and subsidiaries normally found at the back of an American report.

Following these 32 pages are the essays—one on the theme "Growth and Environment: The Need for Restraint," and one comprising the chairman's international

The Hongkong and Shanghai Banking Corporation
Annual Report 1976

35/Annual Reports

survey, or business review.

But the heart of this section are the illustrations. In the past, this report has generally used 12 photos or paintings, one from each of 12 of the countries in which the bank has offices. The selection of the artists from year to year is based on a rotating process that weighs importance and precedence of the bank's facilities in 130-plus cities.

However, when the 12 countries for artistic contribution had been decided upon for the 1976 report and various bank representatives contacted, it became apparent that in some areas there were no professionals capable of producing the quality artwork Steiner was looking for. After a conference with the bank's secretary, a simpler format was evolved to include four widely-separated countries or geographical areas, using three artists from each. In a bit of a turnabout, Steiner was off to England, America, Canada, Japan, and back home in Hong Kong, meeting with artists—rather than the usual situation of contracting artists or photographers and sending them to specified locations.

Each artist was asked to make a personal statement about his or her own environment—both commercial illustrators and fine artists were asked to participate. In some cases, Steiner bought an already-completed painting that met the criteria of theme and quality; in one instance, he art-directed "an excellent draftsman and artist to one of the best pictures of the lot."

As might be expected in dealing with 12 personalities

A theme of environmental conservation sent the designer around the globe to commission 12 paintings from artists in four geographical areas in which the bank does business.

Annual Reports/36

flung far about the globe, there were a few down-to-deadline dramas, but all of the paintings were approved by the bank's chairman for use in the report. For all Steiner's careful instructions and measured diagrams, a few were executed to the wrong proportions, but the designer feels that these were cropped with a sensitive eye.

If the relationship of the theme to the bank's business seems thinly stretched (there is no point made of this bank's financing of pollution-control systems or funding of municipal clean-ups), the paintings presented do suggest that this corporation cares about unbridled growth and its concomitant tax on the environment. While some of the paintings (especially those from the Hong Kong artists) present a fairly objective view of the world, more are sensitive if subtle indictments of a man/nature balance gone awry: A pastoral scene spread beneath the landing gear of a supersonic airliner; snowy egrets whose habitat has been destroyed by a nearby industrial plant; the chaos and color of a modern city as seen from the courtyard of a Japanese temple.

Steiner confesses that when he left for his 23-day art-finding trek around the world, he hadn't a clue as to what the cover would be. By the time he returned, he had a notion of a large "E" painted in the sky. What finally transpired was an isometrically projected, upper-case, serifed "E" set against a white ground. The spaces formed by the drawing lend a three-dimensional quality suggesting

37/Annual Reports

"a maze-like" environment; each space has been filled with a piece from a painting inside. The "E" on the front cover uses elements representing the natural environment; on the back the elements in the "E" are man-made.

Although the report was produced in eight months, only two were devoted to the hardcore design work. Steiner was able to trim costs by printing all the color on one side of the sheet, yet the report does not lack a full-color feel. And although producing a one-volume report was a decision made as much for convenience as for economy, the designer admits that it gave him a good feeling to bring this ambitious undertaking in considerably under budget.

Report: The Hongkong and Shanghai Banking Corporation 1976. International banking. 1976 total assets $13.3 billion.
Design firm: Graphic Communication Ltd., Hong Kong
Art director/designer: Henry Steiner
Illustrators: Anna Pugh, Nigel Holmes, Alan Manham, Shoko Sasaki, Akio Yamao, Shiro Tatsumi, Catherine Loeb, Robert Giusti, David Lam, Liu Sze-keung, Nike Arrighi, King Chia-lun.
Copywriter: Shane Olver
Printer: Dai Nippon
Size: 8" by 10"; 76 pages plus covers
Quantity: 68,000

Annual Reports/38

Cummins Engine

It has not been the policy of these Casebooks to analyze a winning design in terms of its designer as a "personality" in the design community, and, with rare exceptions, designer encomiums have been studiously avoided.

But in discussing the 1976 annual report for the Cummins Engine Company, it is difficult to avoid seeing it as an effective piece of contemporary annual report design bearing the unmistakable signature of its creator, Paul Rand.

The cover of the report is a graphic exercise in the clarion colors which typify this designer's work, with four elements placed one in each quadrant of the cover: a yellow arrow, a blue Cummins "C" (the company's symbol, also designed by Rand), a green "7" and a white "6" are squared off against a warm red background.

The cover idea also completes the series of reports issued quarterly by Cummins during the year—each bore as its cover one of the four elements used for the full year's review. The cover was printed in four flat colors (rather than blends of process colors) because Rand wanted to keep those tones clear.

The feeling of color continues through the book by way of charts—simple graphs whose bars and lines are printed in clear red, blue, green, orange or yellow—and by the establishment of a color-coded strip at the edge of the pages. The book is divided into three sections—text, photographs, and financials—and each has its

39/Annual Reports

own color-strip to provide "visual relief as well as to signal content change."

These colors crop up again in the back of the book, where a three-page pull-out map indicates Cummins' worldwide operations. Each area served by the company is printed in a separate hue (Communist-bloc countries are printed in a medium gray) which overprints a striped, light gray background. Numbers dropped around the map are keyed to a list of operations appearing on the gatefold overleaf. Thus, the map works effectively on levels of both design and information.

Outside of the sparks of color in this report, there is a general feeling of understatement and reserve. Type is Helvetica in light and medium weights; heads are not scaled up but kept to the same point-size as body copy. The text section is organized into two columns that sit to the right of each page, leaving an ample margin to the left; financials are set into a single broad measure that utilizes the same space.

The visual section of this report is a series of photographs, taken by Cummins, of various Cummins-powered vehicles in use around the world. Captions are run ticker-tape-style through full-page photos or between individual ones; the caption strip is the same 2-pica width as the colorstrip at the page edge—a nice correlation.

The opening photo spread is a miniature photo essay centering on one driver, an independent trucker who

Clarion colors in photos, map and graphic device mark this report as the work of Paul Rand.

Annual Reports/40

makes a weekly 1400-mile run between San Diego and Vancouver in his turbocharged, KT-450-horsepower Cummins-engine truck. There is a nice, personal feeling here of real-life trust for a product (the trucker's story is recounted in the operations review text); it is all the more appealing when one considers that this privately-purchased rig sells for $60,000.

Other photographs are no less realistic in their depiction of Cummins around the world —in manufacturing plants, powering pumps in orange groves, buses in Bruges, switch engines in Tokyo, tugboats in Tonawanda. "Photographs," Rand notes, "are simpler, more believable, more economical, and quicker to do"; they also impart a personal feel for Cummins' business.

Report: Cummins Engine Company 1976. Diesel engines, parts and components. 1976 sales $1.03 billion.
Designer: Paul Rand
Photographers: Richard A. Meek, John Terrence Turner, Ike Beverly
Copywriter: Cummins Engine
Printer: Mossberg Printing

Size: 7⅞" by 11"; 46 pages plus covers
Quantity: 30,000

41/Annual Reports

Great Northern
Nekoosa

Designing an annual report for a paper company always presents the challenge of showing the client's product—the paper on which the report is printed—to best advantage. The safest approach is to specify the company's premium grade printing paper, usually a heavyweight coated stock that easily accepts four-color reproduction, and design a report that uses plenty of full-color photography.

More risky is the combining of two or more of the client's papers, for as colors and textures are added, the report hazards a loss of cohesiveness that even the most tyrannical design format is hard put to unify.

In designing the Great Northern Nekoosa report, Norman Perman takes just such a gamble. Walking a tightrope of two paper textures used in four colors and three weights, he manages to keep a balance despite four-color printing in one section, three-color in another, and hot-stamp bronzing on the cover.

The bulk of the report is printed on Nekoosa Artone text, used in white for the operations review and in orange for the endpapers. This paper has a stippled finish similar to that of a fine watercolor paper, aptly enhancing the loosely washed gouache paintings (in full color) and charcoal drawings (in black only) by illustrator Franklin McMahon that illuminate the report.

The organization of visuals and information is along the dual lines so often seen in annual report design. At the

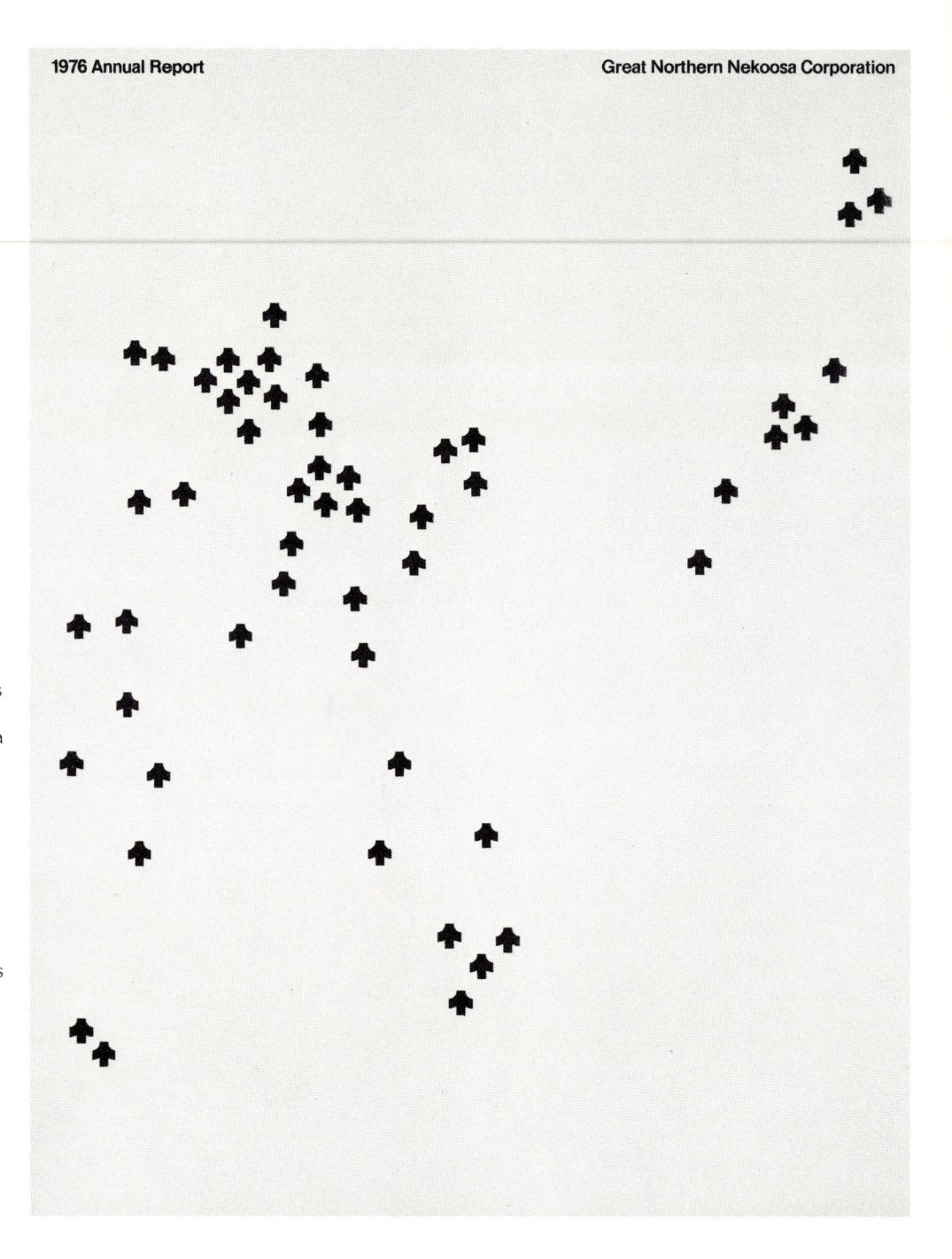

1976 Annual Report   Great Northern Nekoosa Corporation

Annual Reports/42

bottom of the page is a running, three-column text reporting the business year, while above, visuals and captions deal with "papermaking, drawing by drawing." Black line artwork runs across the upper two-thirds of some pages; on others, full-color illustrations run four-corner bleed. Captions for both sit at the top of the black-and-white pages in two columns of seven-point Helvetica Medium. There is one gatefold which offers a three-page, full-color painting of Nekoosa's paper machine at its Millinocket, Maine, installation on one side, and four line drawings of various steps in paper finishing on the other.

The information aspect of this section opens with a stylized map of Nekoosa mills and facilities. There is no outline or other political or geographical indicator on this map—simply the Nekoosa tree symbol in a variety of colors, scattered across the spread, with a tag-line indicator angling off each to locate the site by city and state. Tree colors are keyed to the bottom of the chart— green for paper mills, rust for sales offices and paper distributors, yellow for administrative offices, and blue for other facilities. The configuration of the trees on the spread roughly suggests the outline of the U. S., and thus subliminally imparts to the viewer the notion that Nekoosa does indeed cover the map.

This "map" was one of this report's favorite attributes among Casebook jurors, and for at least one, it was

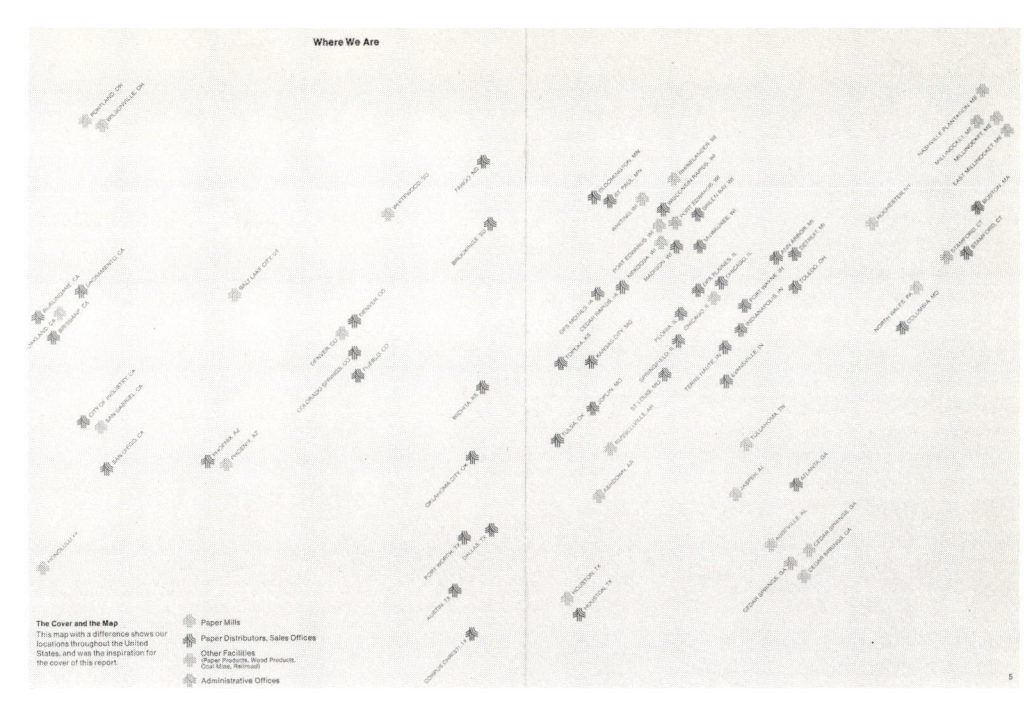

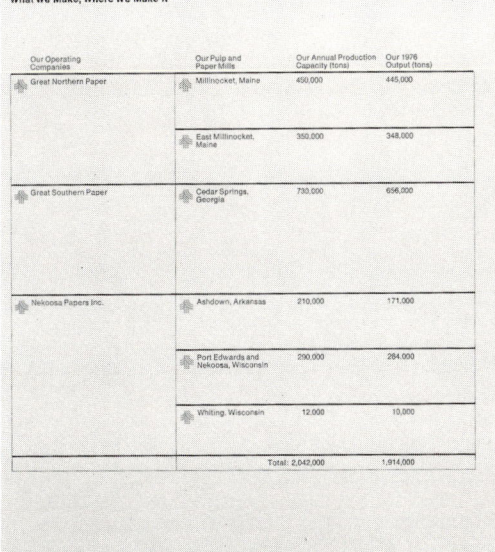

Perman's ace-in-the-hole. But the designer wasn't oblivious to the fact that in this map he had created something special —he chose to wrap it around the cover of the report, too. His original idea of die-cutting the trees to allow the orange endpapers to show through, however, proved too intricate and too expensive. Thus, the map was hot-stamped in bronze, without keys or locators, becoming trees against a snowy field, the fringes of a forest, perhaps. A nice solution to a technical problem.

Following the facilities map inside is a spread with more trees, this time organized within a chart explaining what Nekoosa does and where. The corporation's three operating companies—Great Northern Paper, Great Southern Paper, and Nekoosa Papers—are listed vertically, with comparisons of facilities, capacities, and 1976 output running horizontally. Each entry is studded with a Nekoosa tree.

This chart undoubtedly has been created for the financial analyst, yet the language and presentation are for the layman.

The financial section of the Nekoosa report is printed on two shades of Nekoosa Laureate Laid, using black and sienna on gray for statements and balance sheets, and black and royal blue on tan for the notes and ten-year record. As if this shuffling of paper, texture and color were not enough, Perman takes the last sheet of tan laid and wraps it back to the front of the report, where it holds the letter to shareholders neatly between

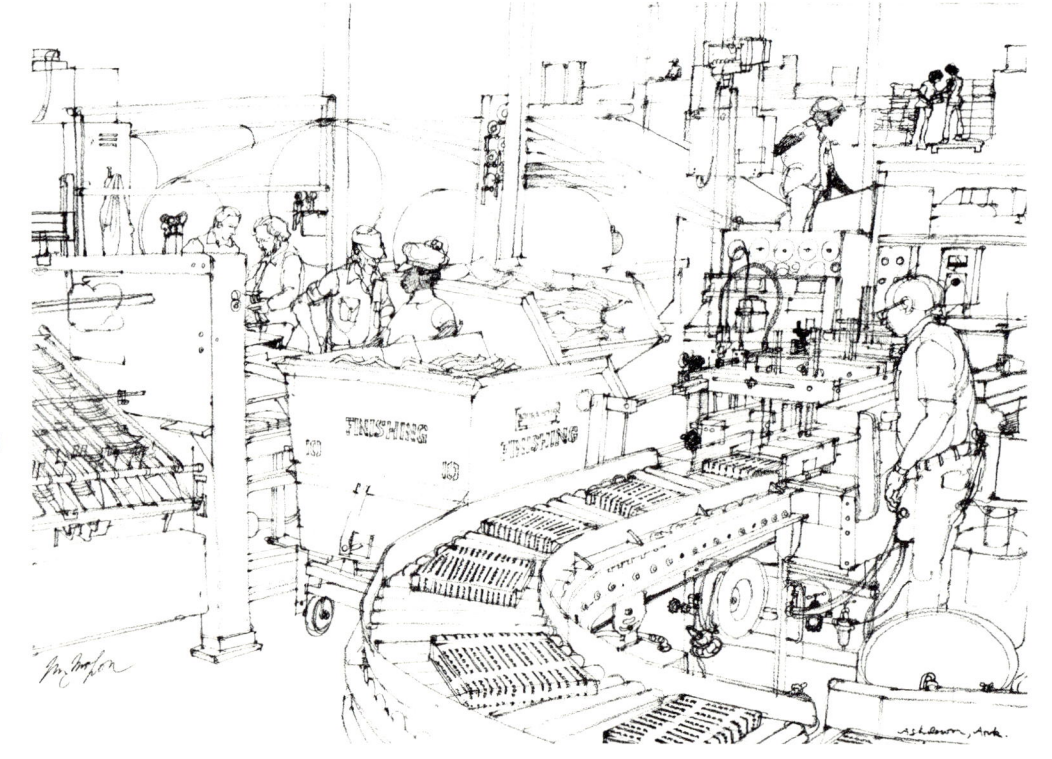

Two papers in three weights and four colors, and a variety of printing techniques, display both product and use for this maker of fine papers.

Annual Reports/44

the orange stippled endpapers and the white-stippled operations review.

Design in the financial section is simple: text and tables are set in broad flush-left, ragged-right columns, one per page. Again, the typeface is Helvetica, in the light weight used for the running text in the operations review. A broad color rule sits at the top of each column; heads and column entries are separated by white space and hairline rules. Here and there, a second color calls out the major factors of income and outgo; charts are simple vertical bars, printed in color, but in keeping with the rather austere mood of the section.

Three additional points here deserve mention. One is the inclusion of Nekoosa's ten-year record; another is a detailed description of paper and production data on the last page. The third is the phenomenally short time in which this complicated annual report was conceived, designed, and produced—in 3½ months, with a budget of $25,000 (including illustrations, excluding typesetting), and with several hundred miles separating the client (in Stamford, Connecticut) and the designer (in Chicago).

Report: Great Northern Nekoosa Corporation 1976. Wood and paper products; coal; railroad. 1976 sales $845 million.
Design firm: Norman Perman, Inc., Chicago
Art director/designer: Norman Perman
Illustrator: Franklin McMahon
Copywriter: Great Northern Nekoosa
Printer: Fine Arts Printing
Size: 8½" by 11"; 44 pages plus endpapers and covers
Quantity: 77,000

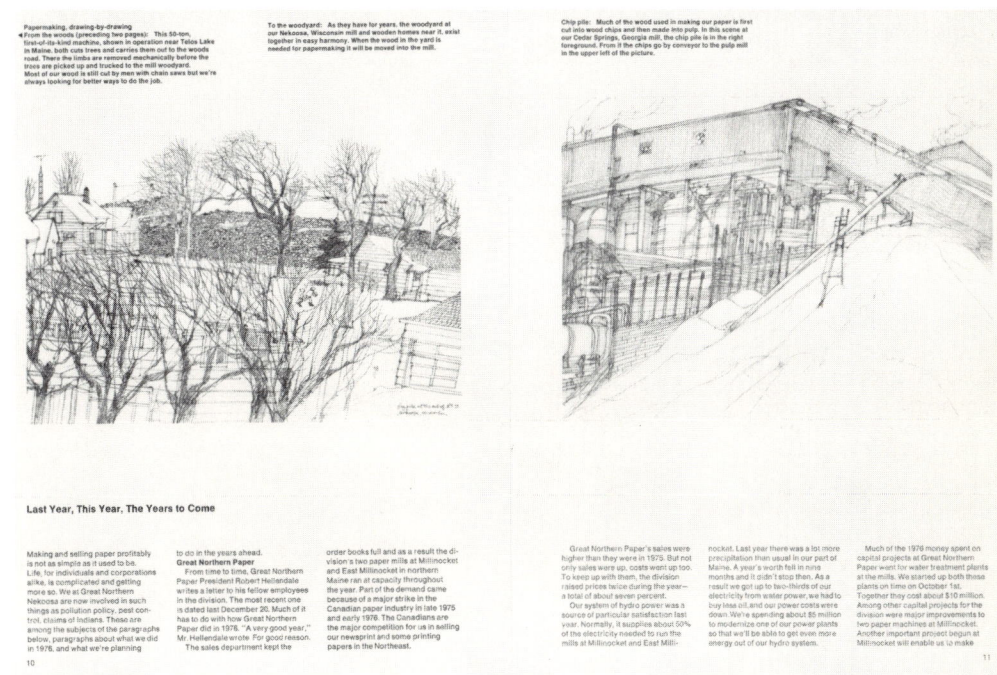

45/Annual Reports

First Boston

Imagine that you are an annual report designer and that one of the most prestigious investment-banking firms in the international financial community calls on you to design its annual report. The report must enhance the image of the company; it must be produced in four colors, for about the same dollar figure as the previous year's two-color report; it must be progressive yet retain elements of taste and appropriateness in keeping with the firm's reputation. You must develop the theme for the report and coordinate design and copy with the firm's corporate communications director. And the report must be in the hands of shareholders in *four months*.

This is not a script idea for "Mission: Impossible"—this was the problem handed to Danne & Blackburn in October 1976 when the designers were asked to produce the First Boston 1976 annual report. This report marks the corporation's first venture into the "designed report" arena (previous ones used all-type solutions), and its first association with Danne & Blackburn.

This report's theme evolves like the lead paragraph of a news story: who manages money at First Boston and what that money does (illustrated with random, four-color spots of the money managers); where the money goes and how (illustrated with four-color spread photographs of First Boston-backed projects), and how much money goes to whom (in a seven-page listing set in three

First Boston 1976 Annual Report

Annual Reports/46

columns of eight-point type per page).

Producing this lavishly understated report in such a short time may have been rewarding for the designers, but their satisfaction was not easily arrived at. Early stages progressed smoothly enough —meetings with the client established a theme and produced a dummy, and with the chairman's approval, photographs were commissioned and production begun. However, because of faulty film manufacture, extensive retouching had to be done on the dye transfers before color separations could be made. Compounding production problems was an eight-year-old court case which was being decided the week the report was to go to press: the designers were forced to pre-print the color photos and strike in text and tables in a separate run.

For all these problems, the finished report reveals not a one. It seems the designers were able to avoid possible trouble spots by certain production decisions. Paper, for example, is Northwest Quintessence in 100-lb. weights for cover and text; its gloss-enamel finish takes excellent four-color reproduction without demanding varnish. The wrap-around cover photo—of an oil refinery financed by First Boston near New Orleans—is backed up on the inside covers with a color block that precludes any show-through. The typefaces used include Times Roman for text and Helvetica Bold for heads — two highly legible faces readily available from type suppliers.

Rice fields in the Philippines are part of the World Bank's many development programs which are helping to improve the economic conditions of poor people in developing countries. First Boston is investment banker to the International Bank for Reconstruction and Development. We are also investment banker to regional development banks, such as the Asian Development Bank and the European Investment Bank, as well as to numerous national development banks around the world. In 1976, we managed development bank issues totaling $2 billion.

Numerous circular fins on each of forty-two gold-plated studs create a "heat sink" which cools the underlying logic chips of a new computer. The L.S.I. chips, each smaller than a postage stamp, are mounted on this multi-chip carrier. Fifty-one carriers form the heart of a large-scale, general purpose computer system that is designed, manufactured and sold by Amdahl Corporation. Founded in 1970, Amdahl made its first public offering last August—an issue of 1,062,500 shares of common stock managed by First Boston. For 1976, Amdahl announced revenues exceeding $92 million.

Lush spread photography and the designers' attention to detail make First Boston's first "designed" report an exercise in lavish understatement.

47/Annual Reports

The design format is simple and straightforward, yet manages to impart a feel for the company and what it does. The report's size—a slightly-larger-than-usual 8½" by 11⅜"—subtly increases its sense of presence. As for visual content, the designers felt that financial transactions needed to have believability and substance, needed to be portrayed by something tangible. Thus, the financial highlights and letter to stockholders are followed by photo spreads that are as different from one another as they are dramatic. A young worker walks one of the many paths winding through a rice field in the Philippines; the caption tells us that, through the World Bank, First Boston assists in one of "many development programs which are helping to improve the economic conditions of poor people in developing countries." A gleaming black and gold metal sculpture set symmetrically across one spread, the caption reveals, is in reality a bit of the heart of a large-scale computer system designed and produced with the help of First Boston. A turbine generator that fairly dwarfs two nearby utility workers fills the next spread; as part of one of the largest nuclear power plants west of the Mississippi, we are told, this generator owes its existence to First Boston. Altruism, progress, service to the public—this is only part of the First Boston story.

Only 17 of this report's 40 pages are devoted to creating an atmosphere for the facts and figures presented in the remainder of the book.

Following the last picture spread are four pages of tabular material, five pages of notes to financial statements, and four with the auditor's opinion and financial review. Then follows the seven-page listing mentioned before—a highly unusual display of issues handled, information not usually made available to the general public. In addition to the mention of various advisory and commercial capacities, there are included here nearly 400 financial dealings in a dozen categories of international and domestic spheres of industry and government, each spelled out in number of dollars raised and date of maturation. The book closes with the usual listing of board members and notes on meetings, transfer agents, and so on.

As the client had hoped, everything about this report says integrity. As the designers had hoped, the report serves to create a strong, contemporary image for the client and, despite trials, was produced on time with a per-copy cost comparable to the previous report.

Report: First Boston, Inc., 1976. Investment bankers. 1976 revenues $110 million.
Design firm: Danne & Blackburn, New York
Art directors: Richard Danne, Bruce Blackburn
Designer: Richard Danne
Photographers: Elliott Erwitt/Magnum; Phil Marco; Edwin Huffman/World Bank
Copywriter: Jeanne Krause/First Boston
Printer: Sanders Printing
Size: 8½" by 11⅜"; 40 pages plus covers
Quantity: 70,000

Bradford National

Bradford National is a young company involved in a period of rapid growth: each year in the past five years has seen an increase in revenues of from 15 per cent to 35 per cent over the previous year. Perhaps it's for this reason that, instead of reading like a typical annual report, this one has the tone and look of a capabilities brochure.

While the report's structure is pure annual report—highlights appear on page one, followed by a letter to shareholders and the business and financial reviews—the style of writing is unique. The operations-review text—and the phrase is used here advisedly—begins with an imposing headline: "Bradford National: Its Vision and Its Goal." Each successive headline begins similarly and outlines the services performed by the company: "Bradford National: Its Services to..." The blank is variously filled in with words like "investment companies and mutual funds," "the securities industry," "government," and so on. Bradford offers computerized transaction and record-keeping to a variety of institutions, and it makes no bones about spelling out those services.

Between the headlines is a large-sized serif text elaborating the various points—there is no need for bifocals in reading this report. Management requested that this type be run large. The choice of a serif face makes the text all the more legible, and it forms a nice balance with the four-color photography, too.

The photographs number only five, but give the feeling

49/Annual Reports

of twice that number. They are run horizontally, so that each spread is comprised of one wide column of text and one photo that begins a couple of inches from the gutter on the left-hand page and bleeds across to the trim on the right.

The photos are of a curious sort. With one clearly focused exception, they are shot with a zoom, or figures are blurring past the shutter, or depth-of-field or camera angle obfuscates part of the picture. These tricks lend a feeling of movement to the otherwise standard "operations" shots, and fit well into the dynamic theme of the report.

Charts, too, have been designed to "reflect as much growth as possible," at the client's instruction. Styled like the tabs on file folders, the charts highlight the four pages of financial review with a visual interpretation of Bradford's upward growth. These are printed in earthy tones of red, green and yellow achieved through the process color used throughout the book.

Another client request was a map of the company's 33 facilities locations placed on the cover. The designer turned this map into a feat of embossing, debossing and tightly registered printing. The effect is that of a computer punch card, with each location indicated by an oblong that suggests the holes read by a computer terminal. The cover solution is dignified and highly in keeping with the company's operations.

In responding to the standard Casebook questionnaire, the designer notes that certain budgetary

managers, many of the Fortune 500 industrial corporations, and some of the largest city, state and federal agencies.

Bradford National: Its Services To Banks
Bradford provides a full range of important services to the Trust and Commercial Banking Departments of banks of every size.

Trust Department
Corporate Trust Services include complete stock and bond transfer services with all processing done in the bank's name to retain and enhance its relationships with its customers. Services include not only the usual registration and transfer of securities but proxy, annual meeting, and shareholder services of many kinds. By using Bradford, a bank's corporate clients can virtually eliminate the need for a New York co-transfer agent.

Unique optional services are provided such as remote stock transfer services through use of terminals on the bank's premises or at a local data center. Bradford also offers a flexible dividend reinvestment service. Its corporate capital reorganization service includes all of the clerical and recordkeeping requirements for mergers, tenders and subscriptions of a bank's corporate customers. Bookshare transfers are made through TAD Depository Corporation, Bradford's affiliated Transfer Agent Depository, a clearing corporation. Personal Trust Services include Bradford's Trust Accounting Services, a totally integrated on-line system for all principal and income transactions executed by the trust division of a bank for its individual customers. The system includes income reconciliation, automatic income disbursement, preparation of tax returns, common trust fund accounting and more. The Trust Accounting Service can also be totally integrated with Bradford's custody services.

Custody Services include the daily processing, receipt, and disbursement of interest and dividends, daily reconciliation of each account, inventory of pending transactions with trade date accounting, as well as the preparation of all daily and other periodic reports. Bradford Trust Company is now a full-service custodian for more than seven billion dollars of the assets of its customers.

In addition, Securities Clearance and Settlement Services are available in major financial centers in the United States through Bradford Securities Processing Services, Inc., a registered clearing agent. Clearance of government securities is facilitated through Bradford Trust Company, a member of the Federal Reserve System. Draft Collection Services are provided, which include shipment of securities and overnight collection of funds on drafts presented at any of Bradford's national facilities.

Commercial Banking Department
Bradford's banking specialists have worked with more than 300 banks to improve the productivity of their data processing, clerical and marketing activities.

broker-dealers utilize Bradford for clearing municipal and corporate bonds, as well as U.S. Treasury and Government Agency securities.

New issues of debt and equity securities are packaged, financed and delivered throughout the nation for underwriting syndicates. As a Transfer Agency Depository, book entry transfer services are made available by a Bradford affiliate for over 2,000 issues, including options, with substantial savings to customers. Stock loan services bring lenders and borrowers of securities together and coordinate the delivery and the return of those securities at significant savings.

For the Trading Department, options trades on the Chicago Board Options Exchange are executed and cleared by Bradford. Full professional correspondent services are provided, reducing the customer's fixed costs.

For the Investment Advisory Department, Security Accounting Services are furnished by Bradford's portfolio recordkeeping systems. These systems include overnight reporting with a full audit trail of each transaction, daily pricing, performance measurement grouped by security category, and much other information needed for the management of the account. Custody Services are provided through Bradford Trust Company. All necessary information is supplied for safekeeping and the daily management and investment of each account.

For the Sales and Marketing Departments, Bradford's Prospect Appraisal Service provides customers with portfolio evaluation by industry category with tax costs, current pricing, and income analysis on each security.

Bradford National: Its Services to Corporations
One of Bradford's largest group of customers is business corporations.

Shareholder and Bondholder Services:
For corporations Bradford provides a full range of shareholder and bondholder services including certificate registration, stock and bond transfer, on-line shareholder information, and increasingly important dividend reinvestment services. Corporate Capital Reorganization Services, which include all the recordkeeping and processing services required for tenders, mergers, acquisitions and rights offerings by corporations, are also provided.

Employee Benefits:
Bradford acts for corporations as directed trustee and custodian for all kinds of employee benefit plans. Services include safekeeping of assets, administration of trusts, portfolio accounting, disbursement of funds to beneficiaries, and all recordkeeping for participants in the plans.

Computer Operations:
Bradford designs large scale computer systems and programs and installs them for business corporations. It also operates computer facilities for business corporations under rigid controls and procedures to insure budgeted and scheduled performance.

NEW OFFICES FOR EXPANDED SERVICES: Located in the heart of Boston's financial district, these new offices of Bradford Trust Company of Boston serve banks, fiduciaries, investment companies, corporations and individuals throughout the New England area.

HIGH VELOCITY PAPER HANDLING: Bradford's services to brokers, dealers, and underwriters reduce recordkeeping and paper-handling costs, quickening the flow of financial data to and from the nation's securities markets.

Annual Reports/50

considerations influenced choice of stock used in the report. Those papers selected also reflect the client's subjective preferences and, for the cover, the rigors of the double-embossing process. This is a lot of annual report for $1.18 per copy, and the designer is well justified in his feeling that, despite client needs, the report maintains a high level of integrity.

Report: Bradford National Corporation 1976. Computerized record-keeping services. 1976 revenues $65.8 million.
Design firm: The Graphic Expression, New York
Art director: Bob Glassman
Designer: Dagfinn Olsen
Phtographer: Bill Farrell
Copywriter: Bradford National
Printer: Record Offset
Size: 8½" by 11"; 32 pages plus covers
Quantity: 30,000

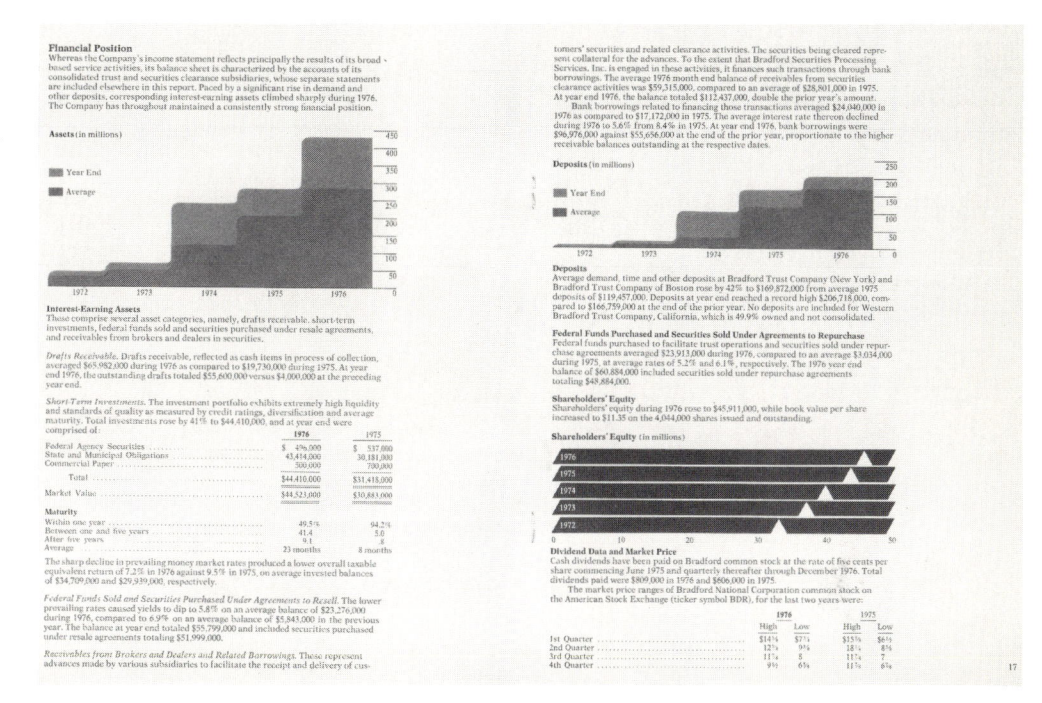

Large type, double embossing and unusual photography create a dynamic feeling that aptly reflects this company's rapid growth.

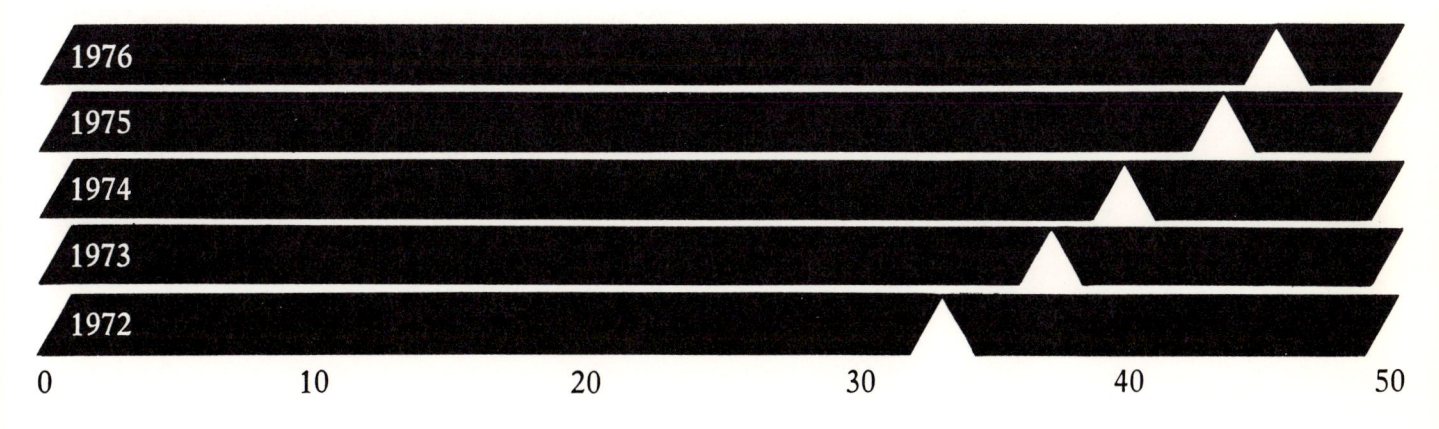

51/Annual Reports

Spencer Foundation

The Spencer Foundation is a fund established with the estate of the late Lyle Spencer, founder of Science Research Associates, which publishes educational materials.

Notes discovered after Spencer's death indicated his feeling that, since the family money had been earned in educational publishing, "much of this money should be returned eventually to investigate ways in which education can be improved around the world." Accordingly, monies in the fund are used to support educational research projects.

It should be noted that there are those who do not feel that annual reports for organizations of this nature should be included in a review of corporate financial documents such as this Casebook. Foundations, hospitals, and the like, are not governed by the same rules as SEC-regulated corporations, nor are their reports intended for the scrutinizing eye of the financial analyst, as are corporate annual reports. However, it is the feeling of the Casebook editors that, inasmuch as the annual report issued by a foundation faces many (if not all) of the same basic design problems as its corporate cousin—the presentation of a year-in-review text, financial statements, possibly the inclusion of photographs, charts or other visual materials—a review of its design process can be an equally instructive exercise.

The two words that come to mind when looking at the 1977 report of the Spencer Foundation are "understated"

Annual Reports/52

and "elegant." Designer Edward Hughes was working within the parameters of a very strict budget; no monies were allotted for photography of any sort nor for photoengraving or separations. The problem, then, was to design an all-type report that would be visually appealing and inviting to read.

The handsome solution came by the exercise of a good deal of restraint, and by the thoughtful selection of the basic components making up the report: a design format that, with its limiting of text to the right-hand two-thirds of each page, incorporates plenty of white space to offset the all-copy presentation; the use of a single typeface— Helvetica—in two weights (light for text, medium for heads); the sparing use of a second color (a rich blue) for rules at page top and bottom, as well as for outsize folios set at the top-left of each column of white space.

Enhancing the restrained design scheme are two weights of papers. Hughes chose a fine-body, medium-weight text for inside pages; the cover is a heavier Mohawk Cover in a soft tan color, with the foundation name embossed across the top. Separating the two weights is a wrap-around Tweedweave endsheet, unprinted, in a rich blue approximating the second color used inside.

For Hughes, the Spencer report "is what design is all about. There are no gimmicks, flashy color, super photos or art to carry it. It is pure typographic design, and either it works, or it doesn't."

The Spencer report works.

Report: The Spencer Foundation 1977. 1977 assets $73 million.
Design firm: Edward Hughes Design, Chicago
Art director/designer: Edward Hughes
Copywriter: The Spencer Foundation
Printer: Rohner Printing
Size: 7¼" by 9-15/16"; 44 pages plus covers and endpapers
Quantity: 8500

Clean typography, well handled— a simple report that works.

53/Annual Reports

Smith International

It was interesting to note during the judging of the annual reports for this Casebook that many of the best reports from both coasts come from a handful of design firms. One of those firms is James Cross Design, a Los Angeles-based design office that works on 20-odd reports a year and has four in this third edition of the Casebooks.

The Smith International 1976 report is the first designed by the Cross office for this client, and it is a gem. Smith International is a maker and marketer of "downhole tools and services"—the drill bits and pipe and other parts and services needed in gas and oil drilling and mining operations.

Obviously, tri-cone insert bits, inlaid bearing surfaces, leg assemblies, stabilizers, and reamers are not items most of us encounter in our daily lives. But products like these have made Smith International a leading supplier to mining and mineral operations, and, beginning with the dramatic close-up of a drill bit on the cover, they form the focal point of this report.

Central to organization of information here is the decision to run text-left/photo-right throughout the operations/business review. The left-hand text page bears two columns of copy centered in the left-hand portion of the page, with broad margins top and bottom. The third column on this page is reserved for one or two smaller photographs and the caption for these and for the photograph that runs four-corner bleed opposite.

The focal point of each

spread is that right-hand photo page—a dramatic shot, often startlingly close up, of one of the company's products. The smaller photos pull back a bit to reveal more of the object shown at right or to show related objects or processes in its manufacture. Added to several of these caption columns is a drawing or two that further clarifies the sophisticated technologies and products.

The color in these photographs sets the pace for the other components of the report. The bright orangey-red of a 1600-degree-heated steel bar, the blue steel of a "kelly" (the bar which applies rotation to the drill from the power source), the rich green of a rotary reamer, the silver-gray sheen of metal drill parts—these colors appear again and again.

The opening spread (inside front cover/page 1), for example, are printed rich blue and true green, respectively, with Smith's "who we are" copy dropped out in white on the right. Page 2 presents a set of handsome charts whose ascenders are pleasingly plump color bars in seven hues that appear later in the photographs.

But one of the most charming (if such esoteric hardware can be so labeled) components of this report are the drawings that sit at the bottom of certain caption blocks. Drawn in accurate line and printed in bright colors, they serve to elucidate text and photos and then reappear as product illustrations in a full-page "Product Groups as a Percentage of Sales" chart. The drawings both serve a

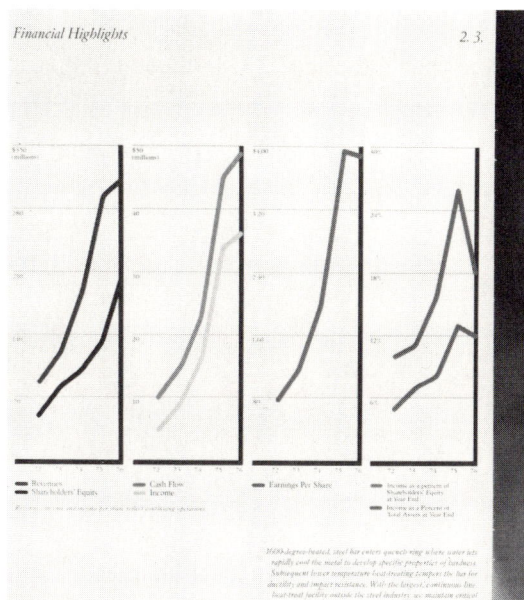

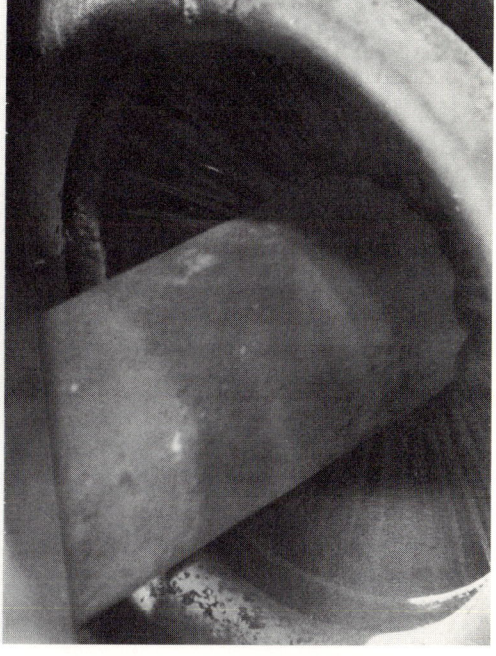

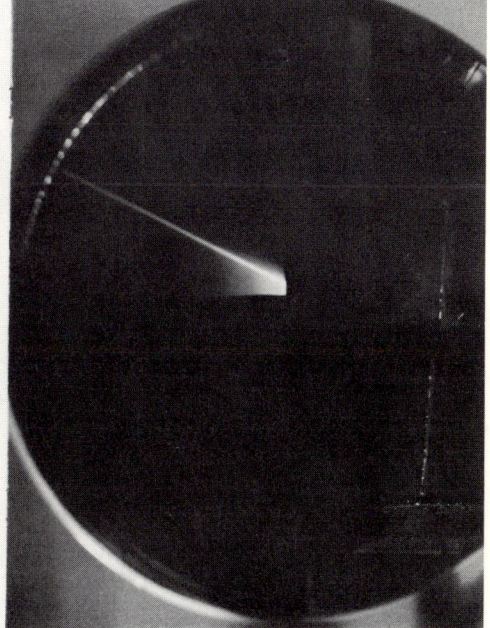

Dramatic close-up photography of esoteric products for oil-drilling and mining operations are explained by colorful diagrams.

55/Annual Reports

purpose and create visual interest here—and are more exciting to look at than the usual pie-chart.

The operations/business review section of this report is printed on a dull-coated stock; photographs are all full-color, and both photos and drawings have been varnished for added richness.

The financial pages of the Smith report are a 20-page form, printed on a buff rag stock and bound separately into the cover. Design here is within the same deep margins set at top and bottom of the operations pages. The same serif face is used, set into the various financial tables with hairline, and here and there double-hairline, rules. The information is neat and approachable.

One more nice touch: Folios throughout the report are set in an oversize italic in the top-right-hand corner of each left-hand page. This effectively solves the continuing problem of what to do with the folios on the right-hand picture pages; and when the facing pages each bear a headline at the top, heads and folios form a neat continuous band.

When so many annual reports use little beyond a formula to achieve an acceptable level of design, it is good to see a report like this one. If Smith, as the designer says, is a company using "sophisticated technologies" to produce products that are "highly specialized rather than commonplace," the designer has gone beyond commonplace "formula" design to achieve a report that is as appealing as it is sophisticated.

Report: Smith International, Inc. 1976. Drill bits and other tools and services for mining and industrial applications. 1976 revenues $308 million.
Design firm: James Cross Design Office, Los Angeles
Art director/designer: James Cross
Photographer: Jayson Hailey
Copywriter: Smith International
Printer: Gardner Fulmer Lithograph
Size: 8½" by 11"; 49 pages plus covers
Quantity: 25,000

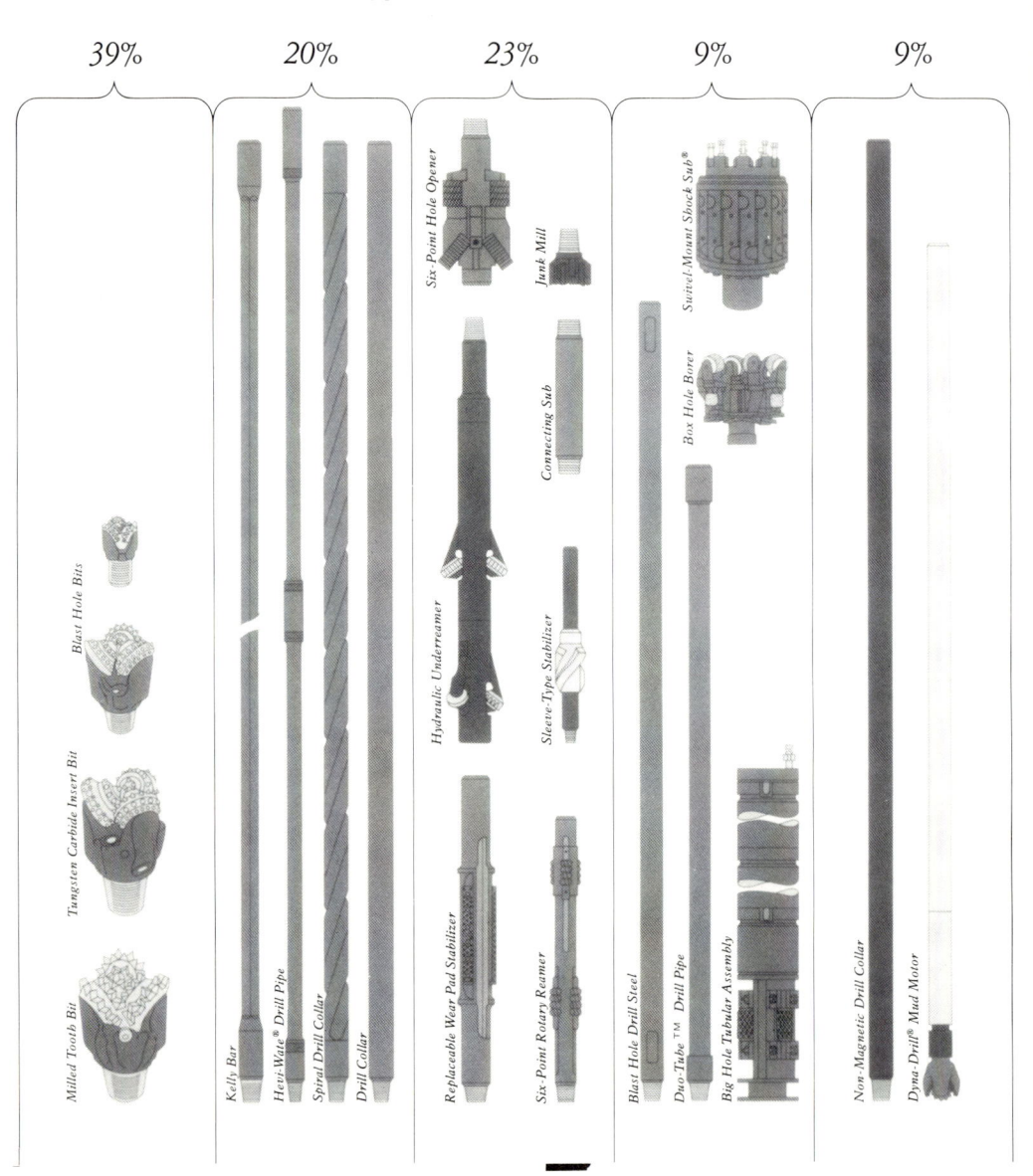

Annual Reports/56

Manufacturers Hanover

This is the third report designed by Harrison Associates, a design firm located in suburban New York, to appear in the Annual Report Casebooks, and it is significantly different from the earlier winners.

While the two previous Harrison winners were first-rate examples of the traditional well-designed annual report—including beautiful full-color photography centering on products and people—the Manufacturers Hanover report is printed primarily in black-and-white, with here and there a second color used to highlight a headline or, interestingly, a folio.

At the request of the client, the report focuses on clear, dignified portraits of selected employees who represent different areas of bank operations. Since financial institutions have a hard enough time depicting their intangible services, this device is as good as any to suggest the bank's range of capabilities.

But what makes these portraits unique is their presentation. Rather than the full-page bleed photos so often seen in a "people" report, this book uses group shots arranged horizontally across the page or, in some cases, across the page and the gutter and onto the adjoining page. (In two instances, the portrait is an extreme vertical formed when the standard 41-picas-deep photo is run across only two columns of a four-column page.)

Whatever the picture's proportions, each is a carefully designed grouping of

57/Annual Reports

characters. Some are grouped around benches or tables; others flank computer terminals; still others take positions along the railings and banisters of a stairway. While such placements might have had all the appeal of a high school yearbook, these portraits go beyond the simple depicting of people. There is obvious attention paid to setting, background and detail: nothing drifts into or out of focus; there are no tricks played with the camera's depth-of-field. The result is a series of portraits as dignified as the client had hoped for, yet with a certain power and dynamism uncommon in such contrived shots.

But more unusual than the photos are the keys Harrison devised to identify the individuals in the groups. Obviously, certain of these employees have a superior place in the bank's hierarchy, and captions had to reflect the distribution of power within the banking division represented. But how to list the highest-ranking officer first in the identifying copy block—which would ordinarily mean posing that person to read first, left-to-right—without sacrificing the artful designing of the photographs?

The photo-key solves this problem by presenting a three-step picture-reading process. One looks at the picture to see the individual, refers to the key—a schematic outline of the figures portrayed—to find the person's identifying number, then refers to the copy block to see who the person is. It is an intricate, attention-getting device that works, despite the fact that it is

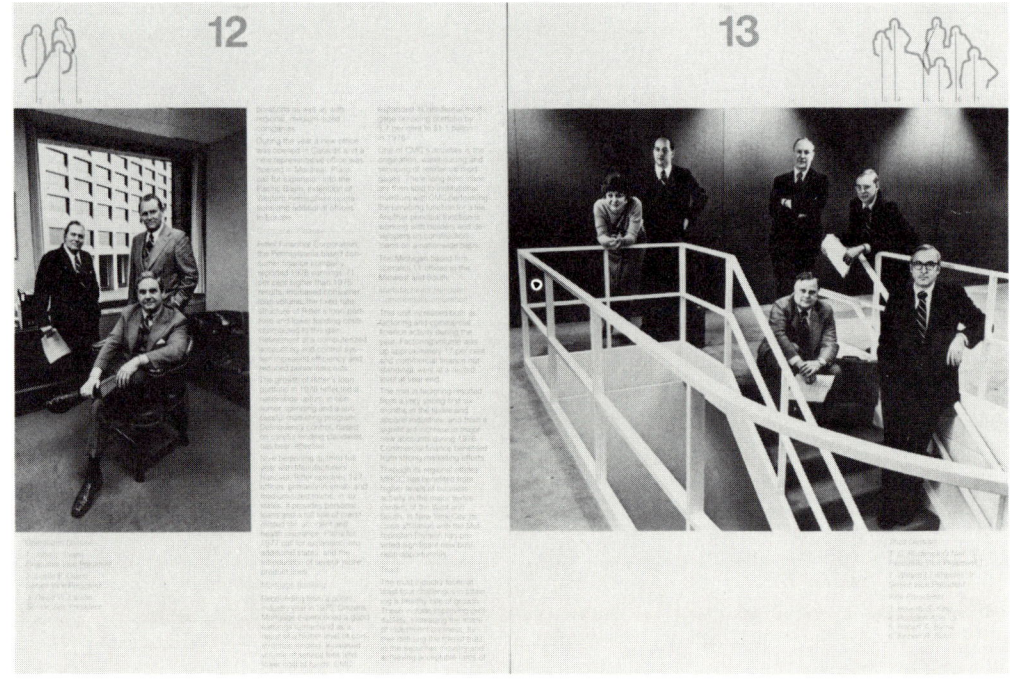

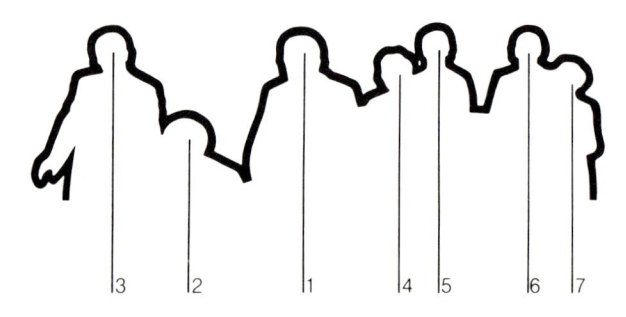

Annual Reports/58

time-consuming and perhaps a bit idiosyncratic.

The rest of this annual report takes a back seat, from a design standpoint, to the portraits. Operations text is presented around the photographs in narrow columns that complete a four-column grid. Charts are simple vertical bars that appear below certain of the photos; they are printed in a soft gray used in the duotone printing of the portraits. This is the same gray used for the photo-keys and for the outsize folios that appear at the top of each page. In the operations section, a clear red is used to call out headlines between the soft-spoken text—also printed in gray.

The remainder of the book is comprised of two sections differentiated by content and paper. The financial review immediately follows the operations text and is printed on khaki Carnival Groove. Two colors are used here— black for copy and figures and a rich blue for the large folios and the rules between tabular entries. The grooves of the paper form an interesting pattern with the tables of figures, helping to separate their tightly set columns one from another.

The last section of this report is an eight-page directory of Manufacturers Hanover officers, subsidiaries and banking offices. These are printed in black on a yellow kraft stock; again, a second color is used for folios and category identifiers—this time, clear red.

Annual report design is an area where one sees little in the way of innovation and experimentation. It is even less often that as conservative an organization as a bank will depart from the safe, "good design" solution. So it is especially refreshing to see a banking report that departs from the four-color-glossy-stock norm with a design that is unusual, dignified—and gently colorful.

Report: Manufacturers Hanover Corporation 1976. 1976 assets $31.5 billion; net income $143 million.
Design firm: Harrison Associates, Port Washington, NY
Art director: Peter Harrison
Designer: Jay Tribich
Photographer: Arnold Newman
Copywriter: Manufacturers Hanover
Printer: Herst Litho
Size: 8½" by 11"; 60 pages plus covers
Quantity: 150,000

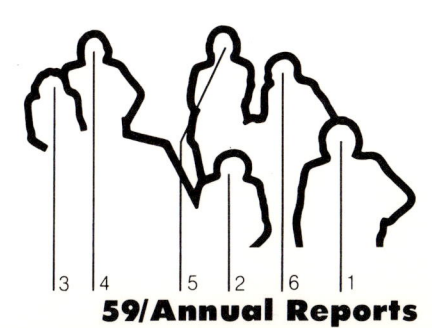

This report focuses on people— through carefully designed group portraits and an arresting series of identifying keys that serves as a graphic theme throughout.

59/Annual Reports

Northrop

Nineteen seventy-six was an important year for Northrop: for the first time, net sales broke the billion-dollar mark. But despite the good track record, Northrop, like other aerospace corporations, faces some public distrust that dates back to the Lockheed debacle of a few years ago.

Northrop goes a long way toward counteracting that loss of faith with this annual report. There is an overall feeling of sophistication and grace about it—what Casebook juror Don Shanosky called "an elegant reserve." This aura is achieved by design—by a conscious effort on the part of the designer to "show the high technology and craftsmanship of Northrop's products in a simple, straightforward way."

Like most annual reports, Northrop's is a combination of typography, photography, fine paper and good printing. Typography here is an up-sized serif face that, along with the two-point rules separating heads and texts, lends the feeling of a classic financial document. The paper is a dull-coated premium grade with the richness of velvet; it is printed in four colors—black and three match—plus a dull varnish for topping off the photographs.

And the photographs! The designer understates their power when he says that they express "quality, precision, and craftsmanship," for it is their expression of Northrop products in such highly sculptural, futuristic terms that makes this report the distinguished piece of communication it is.

The detailing and dramatic lighting of products for annual

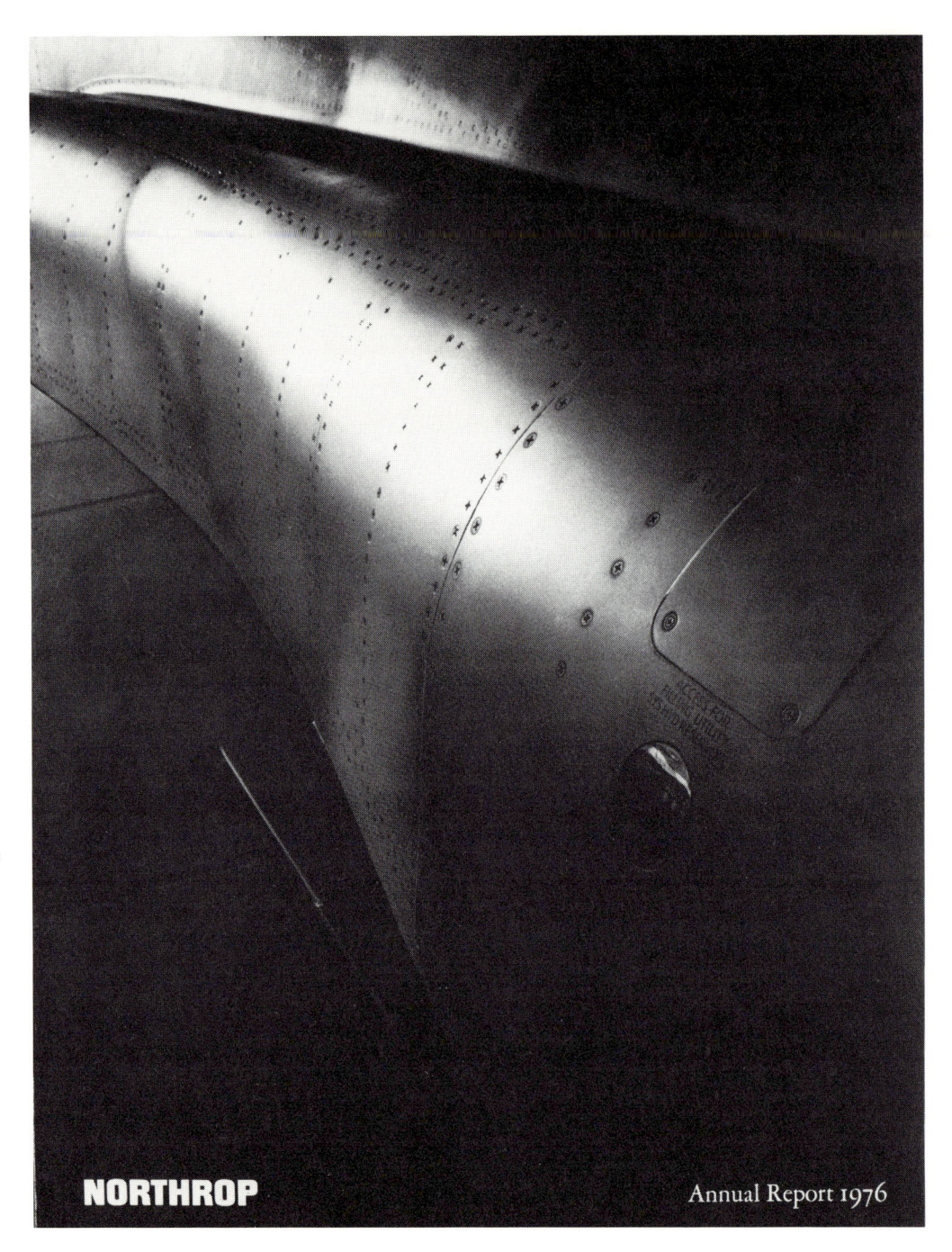

Annual Reports/60

report photography is not new. What makes these photos so spectacular—although they are all printed in black and gray—is a combination of subject matter—the streamlined, aerodynamically engineered bodies of aircraft, and the technologically dazzling aerospace instruments—with the designed use of the camera in presenting it.

The fuselage of Northrop's F-5 Tactical Fighter, for instance, is seen as an example of aerodynamic contouring, an unidentifiable portion of the gleaming aircraft curving seductively across the page. A "wing leading edge extension," photographed in silhouette on a U.S. Navy prototype, is a study in light and shadow. The sheen of brushed metal in an antenna system, a low-angle profile of a transmission circuit board, an extreme-angle shot of a radar-guided, air-to-air missile—even a circular walkway entry in a sports stadium (representing Northrop's construction capability)—are all monuments to precision.

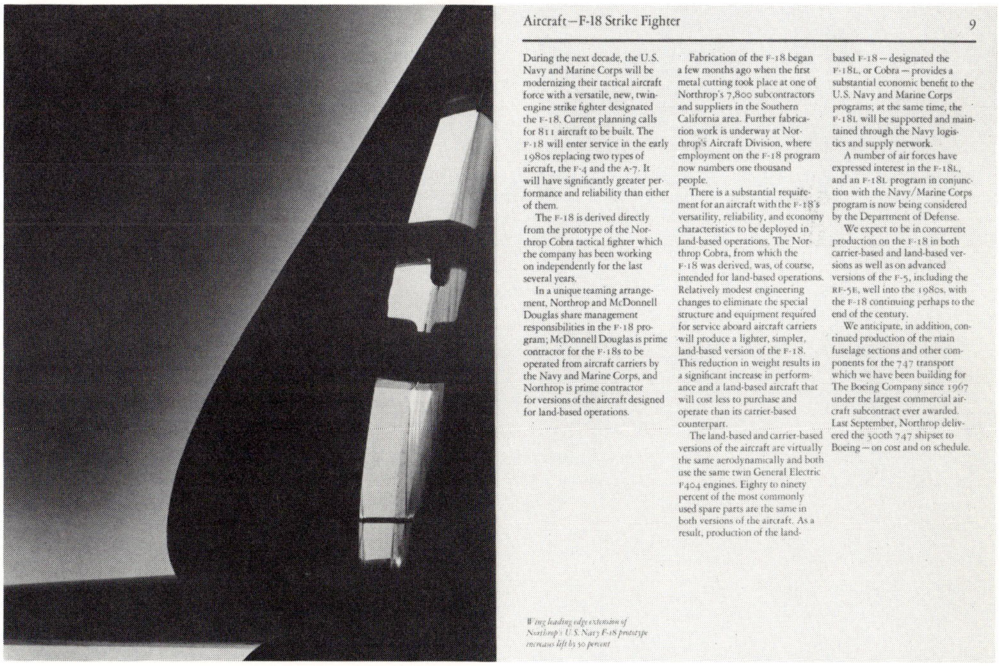

One would suppose a company like Northrop that is involved in military/defense contracts would be cautious about showing its products too well. Yet these photographs manage to impart a feel for that quality and precision the designer hoped to convey, without violating company (or national?) security, and the report as a whole says that, just as Northrop is in control of its manufacturing operations, it is also in control of its future. For the future is very evident in these photographs.

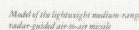

Through futuristic photography and lush duotone printing, aerospace craft and instruments become monuments to precision.

61/Annual Reports

One tends to be so overpowered by the photographs in this report that it comes as somewhat of a surprise to discover that, in addition to the duotone used to print them, there are two other colors that make an appearance. One—a rich sienna—is used on the picture spread for the rule that separates heads from texts. This color reappears along with a cobalt blue and the duotone gray on the various graphs that appear in the financial highlights on page one, and in the more extensive financial report at the end of the book. The charts are simple vertical bar graphs, printed in solids or screens of the various colors, either individually or combined. This decision to add color to the charts helps them hold their own against text and photography.

Designer James Cross notes that, at the outset of this job, there were considerably more, and more complicated, charts to be included—as well as more text. Cross worked with the writer to eliminate redundant areas of copy and with management to eliminate some of the graphs. Northrop's chairman, he notes, "wanted a simple and more powerful layout; thus all complexity was eliminated" in early planning stages. Also deleted were the smaller, full-color photographs that appeared in early proposals.

So it was this judicious editing in the design process—and the exercise of some restraint—that produced a beauty of a report, as well as a feeling of substance and dignity.

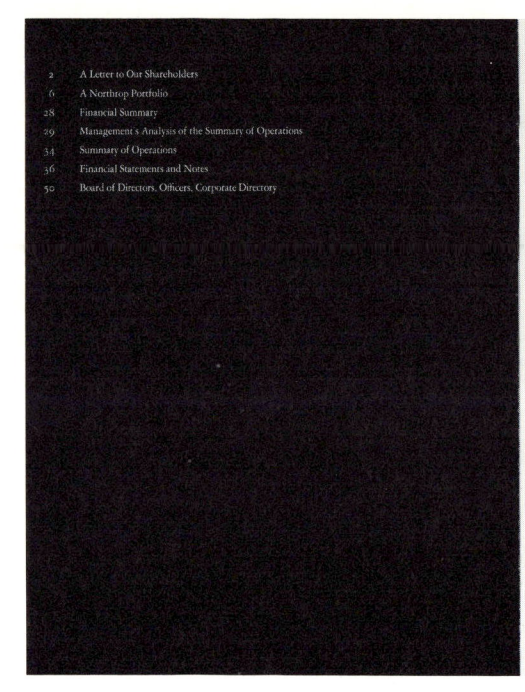

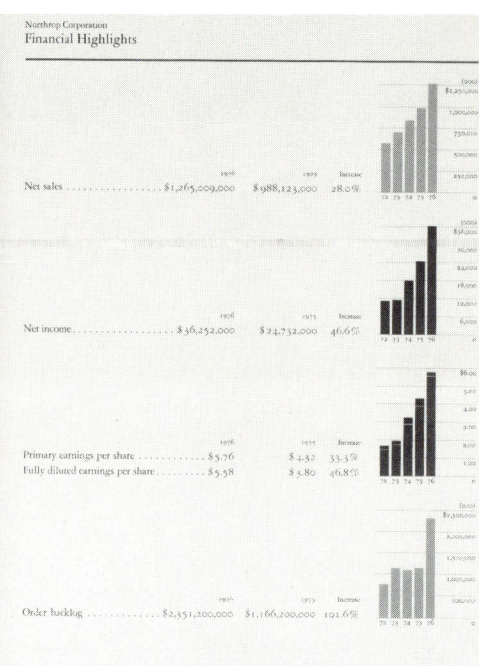

Report: Northrop Corporation 1976. Aerospace design, engineering and fabrication; building construction. 1976 sales $1.3 billion.
Design firm: James Cross Design Office, Los Angeles
Art director/designer: James Cross
Photographer: Per Volquartz
Copywriter: Northrop
Printer: Graphic Press
Size: 8½" by 11"; 52 pages plus covers
Quantity: 75,000

Annual Reports/62

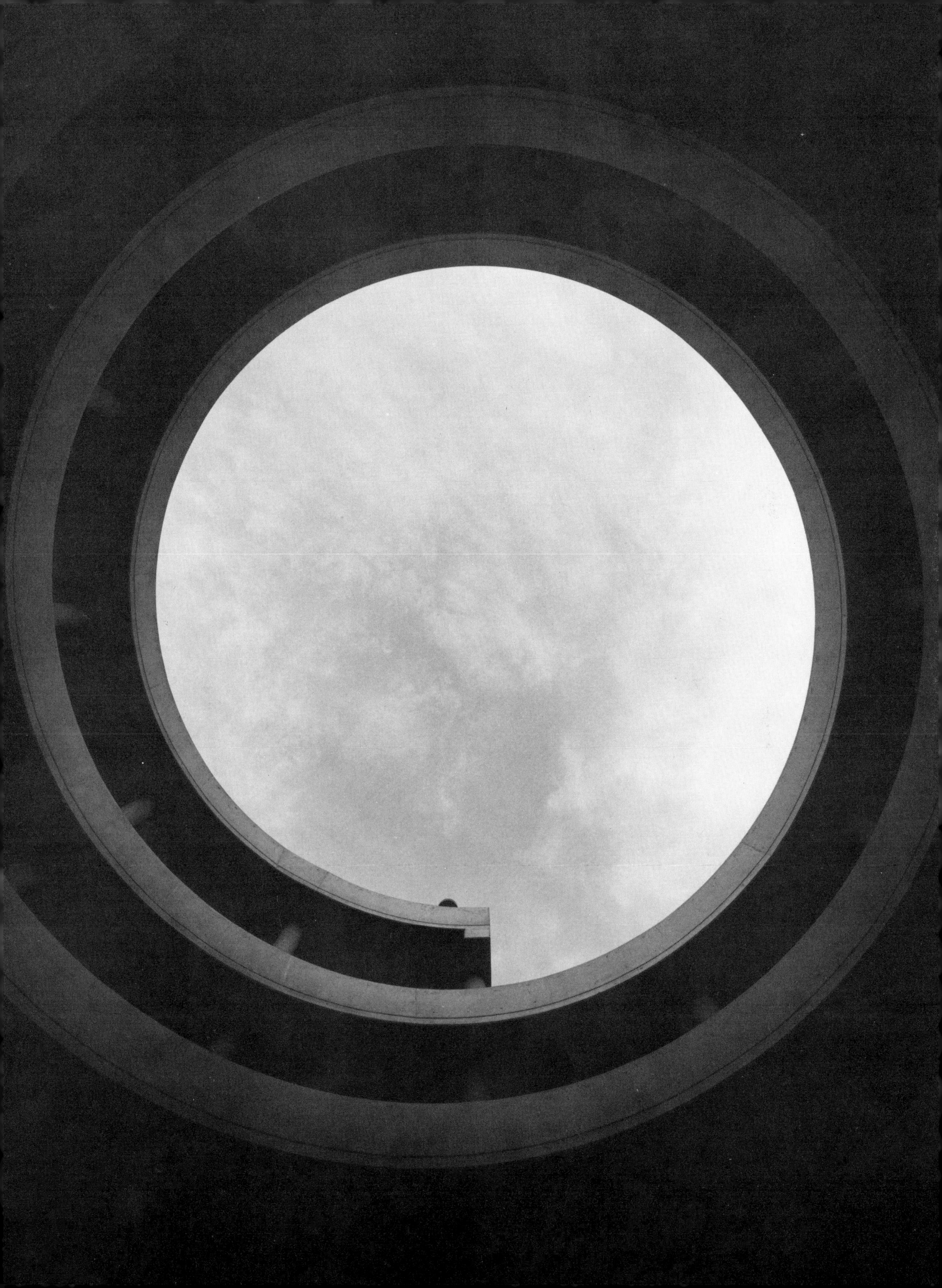

Champion International

As Casebook juror Don Shanosky mused while looking over the Champion International 1976 annual report: "Why change success?" His question was rhetorical, of course, but was a fitting comment on a report whose design is not very different from that of its two most recent predecessors—both of which appeared in the second edition of the Annual Report Casebook. In addition, this report was one of the two that received the votes of all the jurors during this year's Casebook competition.

This report continues the clear image established by Richard Hess in designing Champion's previous two reports. The format dates back to 1974, when Champion underwent a considerable management change and took a right-turn in overall business strategy. Champion, at that time, had been involved in other enterprises besides its mainstay, forest-based operations, and decided to divest itself of its non-forest, non-domestic operations. A consistent annual report format was devised to stabilize the company's image in the financial community.

Like those earlier reports, this one is a perfect-bound 7" by 11" survey of the company; it is written to both the analyst and the casual reader in a language as free from "corp-speak" as possible. Like the others, it is divided into various sections by papers that differ in texture, finish and color, although there is some flexibility within these sections year-to-year.

The 1976 report introduces a new element in what is by now a traditional format. The book opens—after the standard summations and table of contents—with an "at-a-glance" calendar of the business year, taken across two spreads in convoluted, almost whimsical style.

As the second complete year of business since new-management takeover, 1976 was a big year for the company. The calendar offers an illustrated summation of more than 15 major corporate actions, chronicled month-by-month. It is an ingenious piece of design, with spritely drawings and what look like photos clipped from old magazines spotted in seeming disarray across the page. The disarray, of course, is calculated to get the attention of the reader, to say with visual gesturing, "Look what an exciting year we've had!"

The standard first-section for a Champion report is one called "corporate resources," and it is the most flexible in terms of content. The 1975 report focused on trees and their uses; this one focuses on forest lands, pictured in full color.

But resources for Champion includes people. Here, its own "top forty" management personnel are listed, of whom 17 senior corporate officers and operating chiefs are singled out through a series of spot photos—four per person—having the effect of film frames as the gestures and expressions of the faces change. The SEC requires a listing of officers in every report, and this is a bright and innovative solution.

After the "resources" section, the annual report

Though this report follows the design format established by Richard Hess for Champion's previous two annual reports, it retains vitality and freshness.

Annual Reports/64

65/Annual Reports

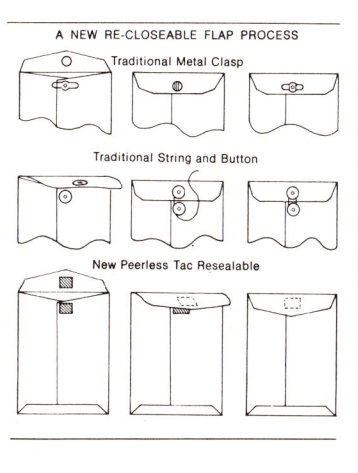

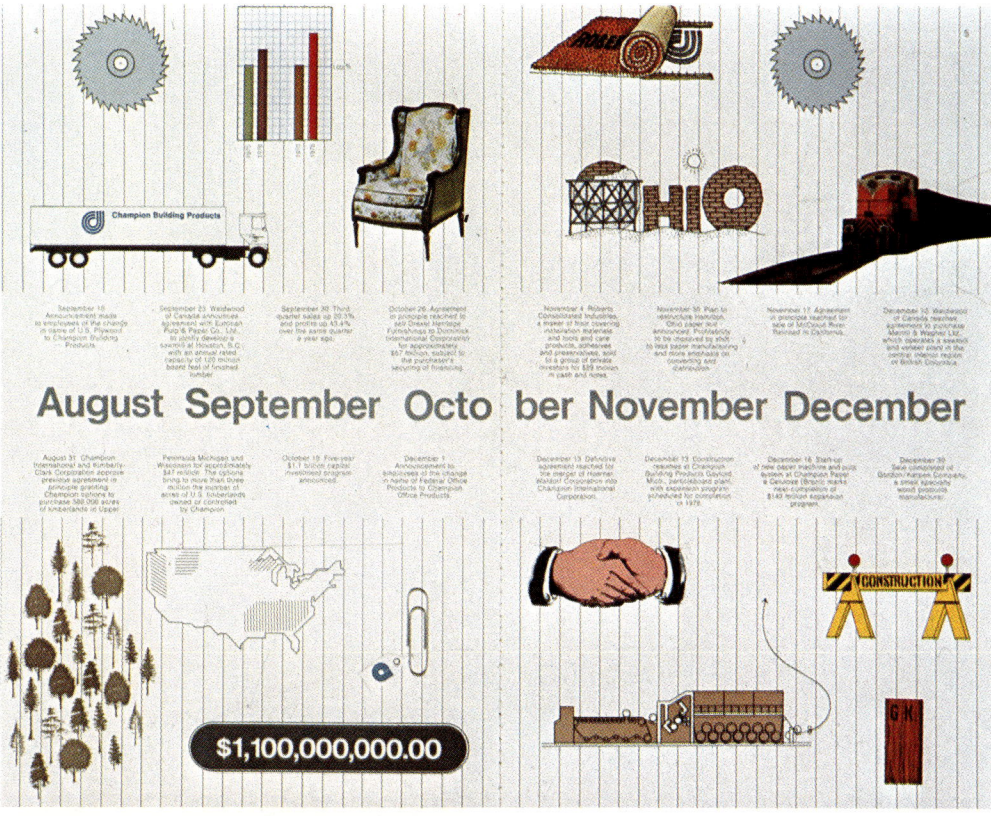

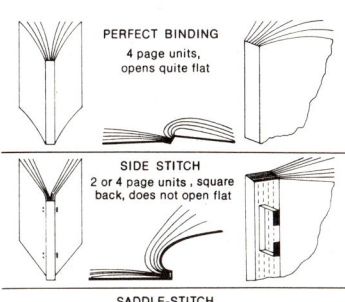

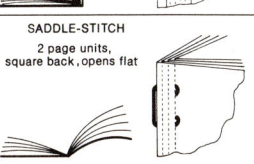

proper begins—a series of sections devoted to each of Champion's product areas or operations line. Here are full-page, glossy photos of Champion goods—in manufacture, being transported, or as they are finally used. Text is printed on a smooth offset stock, with copy detailing the significant events of the year for the particular division and offering an outlook for the future. As in the previous Champion reports, there are plenty of line drawings interspersed with the text to illustrate and explain various product details and processes.

Dividing the sections are sunshine-yellow sheets of Champion's own Carnival Groove; the last section—the financial report—is organized into broad columns of tables and text and is printed on a putty-colored, vellum-finished Carnival Offset. In all, six different papers are used in the report, with the covers being 9-point Colorcast in a vibrant green outside, Chinese red inside. Following form, the Champion symbol and corporate name are embossed on the front.

One would expect to grow tired after three years of so conscientiously applied an annual report format. And yet this third report in the Champion series is as fresh and lively as the first.

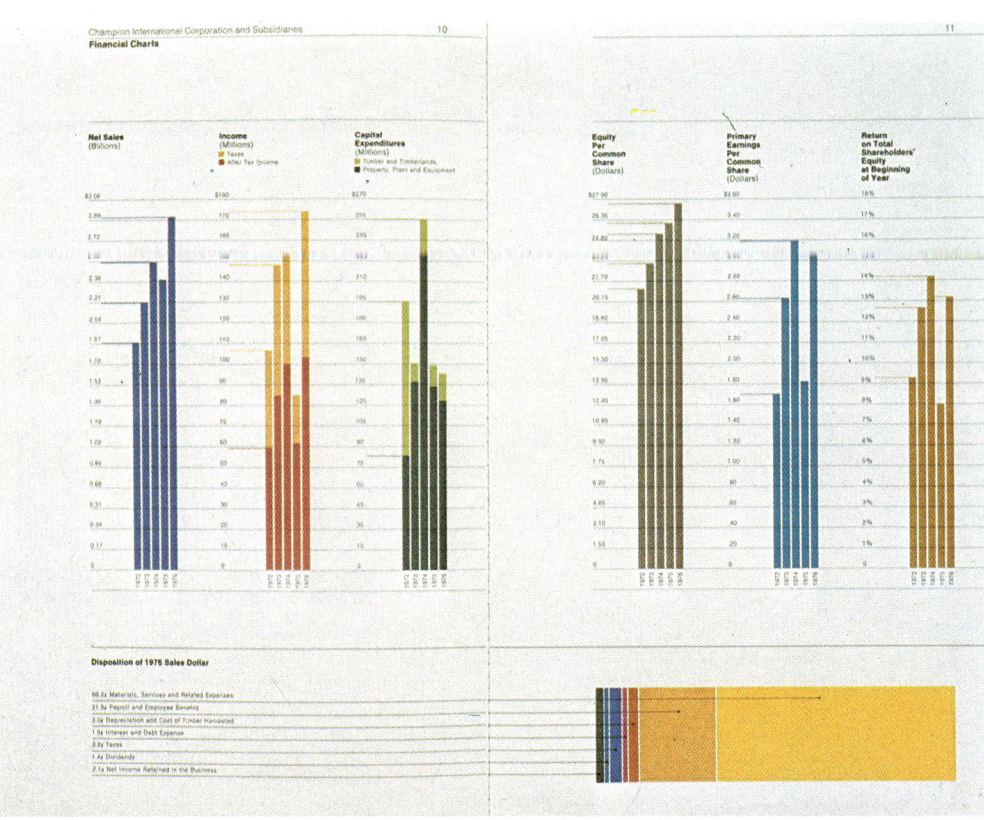

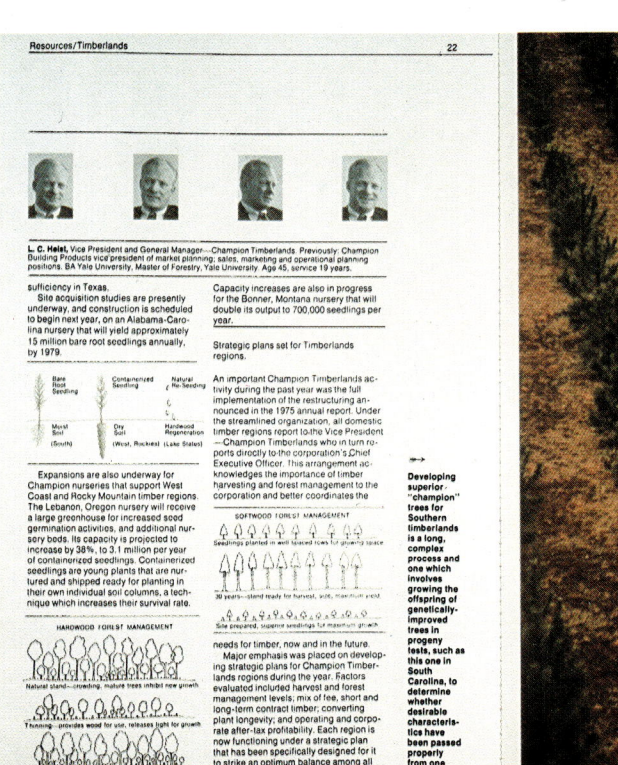

Report: Champion International Corporation 1976. Building materials, pulp and papers, furnishings. 1976 sales $2.9 billion.
Design firm: Richard Hess, Inc., New York
Art director/designer: Richard Hess
Photographers: Werner Wolf/Black Star, Sonja Bullaty & Angelo Lomeo, George Haling, John Lewis Stage, Simpson Kalisher, David Langley, Tom Hollyman
Copywriter: David R. Brown
Printer: Case-Hoyt
Size: 7" by 11"; 68 pages plus covers
Quantity: 100,000

Annual Reports/66

Standard Brands Paint

Do words like "fun," "friendliness," and "whimsy" belong in the parlance of annual report design?

Don Weller thinks so. And these are the very qualities he hoped to instill in the 1976 annual report for Standard Brands Paint Company.

Weller has been designing Standard Brands' reports for six years, so it seems that he has the complete faith and trust of his client. In the 1975 report—also a Casebook winner—his visual theme consisted of a series of photographs in which a white-suited mime transformed a white room into a colorful environment with the help of Standard Brands products.

Like that report, this one seeks separate solutions for text and visuals. While the text is styled as a running report, images are a series of right-hand, full-color, varnished bleed photographs that visualize various facets of the company—manufacture, warehousing, retailing, home improvement and business outlook.

But these are not the typical shots of machinery and the people who operate it, not views of trucks at the loading dock, nor of customers poring over paint chips and wallpaper books. Each photograph is a still life of a few Standard Brands products gathered around the central one—the can of paint.

The element of whimsy in this report comes in two modes. One has to do with that central paint can. The label of the can—or cans—has been illustrated with a scene or with objects that relate to a facet of business being

Standard Brands Paint Company Annual Report 1976

67/**Annual Reports**

discussed in the caption opposite. Thus, the opening photo is illustrated with paint dropping down from the sky to color a predominantly green landscape; the illustrated cans depicting "transportation and warehousing" show pallets of paint cans and a trailer-truck that wraps around two labels; the do-it-yourselfer is represented by seven "portrait cans" grouped around the original landscaped one.

That central can is also the vehicle for a little story-telling. The cover shot of a clean, colorless town with a paint brush sweeping a path of color across the sky, the designer writes, says, "Here comes a fable." The use of illustration reinforces the idea of a paint company, and using the illustrations inside a photograph is both fun and memorable. Of course, the fable—the adding of color to one's life—is completed in the last photograph: the paint brush is gone, and the once colorless town is now bright and cheerful.

The other mode of whimsy here has to do with charts— the brown, Tootsie Roll-shaped devices on the report's first spread—and with the similarly-drawn initial caps used throughout the operations text. While the appropriateness of this kind of trendy motif might be questioned (perhaps stacks of paint cans would have been less startling as graphs, or initial caps drawn in the vein of the Palatino body copy), the designer notes that the charts were drawn to resemble the caps, and the caps were designed to be "bold, soft-looking and dimensional-

Annual Reports/68

feeling" so as to provide the pages of text with "some bold spots of friendliness."

So here we have a report that works together, separately. While it is common in annual report design to use a photo/caption track complementing a text/chart track, the two tracks usually run parallel. This solution runs its tracks at tangents—one is serious and urbane, the other is light and whimsical. The client gets a report that meets the requirements of the financial community, and the designer gets "a touch of spice."

Incidentally, reviewing this year's Standard Brands report was again made more enjoyable by Weller's responses to the questionnaire that is sent to all Casebook winners. Concerning the time allocated for the assignment, he writes: "I began thinking about it when last year's was done. I began being nervous about it on August 1. Layouts were presented and approved by early September and the report came off the press by mid-December."

As to working methods: "I first brought up the idea in a phone call. We work out of Connecticut during late spring and summer and the client is in Los Angeles. The phone allows me to inject enthusiasm into my proposal that a letter can not. (I can yell and stamp my feet)." When the thumbnails, layouts, paste-ups, proofs and final copy have been approved, he adds, "then we go skiing."

And in commenting on the use of illustration, Weller says, "Illustration can add a personal warmth to a report that photos seldom do. Probably 95 per cent of annual reports use photography, and well-designed, clean ones often look perfect and beautiful, but they can look like no human was involved. Illustration reminds us: A human did this!"

and in addition to some meaningful reductions in transit related breakage, it also resulted in a vastly improved loading and unloading operation. In the coming year an increased number of loads will be shipped to our retail outlets on pallets.

Warehousing has long been an important factor in the success of the Company. Our ability to purchase and store unusually large quantities of goods has enabled us to obtain some merchandise in amounts larger than most other companies might want to handle, thereby realizing substantial economies. In addition, we have been able to maintain a year-round flow of imported items which normally require long purchase lead times and in many cases we have been able to offset either shortages or price increases by our ability to "stock up."

RETAIL PAINT AND DECORATING CENTERS. For the most part a trip to a Standard Brands Paint and Decorating Center is made on a well known boulevard into a major shopping area. The outlets are generally located at busy intersections, and are serviced by Company controlled parking areas which are adjacent to the stores. The stores themselves have brightly lit, cheerful interiors that are stocked with a vast variety of home decorating products. Because of the Company's specialization in the home decorating field, it is possible for the stores to offer an unusual depth of product selection in each individual line, thereby enhancing the image of a specialty store in addition to that of a discount operation.

There are currently a total of sixty-three retail centers in our chain. Twenty-four of these centers average 16,000 square feet of retail selling space and encompass a complete carpet department. In these locations carpeting is available for immediate pickup while in the 39 smaller locations which average 11,000 square feet, most carpet must be special ordered from our warehouse.

Due to our high degree of public acceptance, new stores have traditionally become profitable within the first year of their operation. In every phase of store operations, the concentrated emphasis on customer service is apparent. Since most of our customers have little technical knowledge in the home decorating field, "do-it-yourself" experts staff each store and are available to wait on every customer. Their expertise enables them to offer professional advice on any problem arising from a customer's particular decorating project.

PRODUCTS. With the exception of our special order decorator department, all of the 9,200 items we sell in our retail centers are carried in quantities large enough to fulfill most of our customers' home decorating needs. In addition, every effort is made to insure completeness of product lines in terms of color selection, type of product, and price category and every item is sold at prices that are discounted below the prevailing market. All of the paints we manufacture and many of our other products are packaged under Company labels, which due to extensive advertising and customer satisfaction are among the best known in our trading area.

Our special order decorating department provides books and samples of high style wallcoverings, floorcoverings, and other products that are not carried in stock. Here even the most discriminating customer can find just the "right" pattern and have it special-ordered directly from our warehouse or the manufacturer. Generally our marketing emphasis is on merchandise that appeals directly to the do-it-yourselfer. These items feature the most advanced ease of installation properties, such as one coat coverage and water clean-up paints, pre-pasted and pretrimmed wall coverings and self-adhesive and foam backed floor coverings.

CUSTOMERS
Our customers are, for the most part, non-professionals in the home decorating field. They come to Standard Brands Paint Company for selection, sales service, qualified personnel, excellent quality, and prices that are discounted below the prevailing market. In fiscal 1976 we served approximately 15 million customers.

This mix of whimsy and urbanity suggests that two tracks running divergently can indeed end up in the same place.

Report: Standard Brands Paint Company 1976. Manufacture and retailing of paints, wallpapers, carpeting and home decorating products. 1976 sales $135 million.
Design firm: The Weller Institute for the Cure of Design, Los Angeles.
Art director/illustrator: Don Weller
Designers: Don Weller, Chikako Matsubayashi
Photographer: Stan Caplan
Copywriter: Sheldon Weinstein
Printer: Anderson Lithograph
Size: 8½" by 11"; 20 pages plus covers
Quantity: 15,000

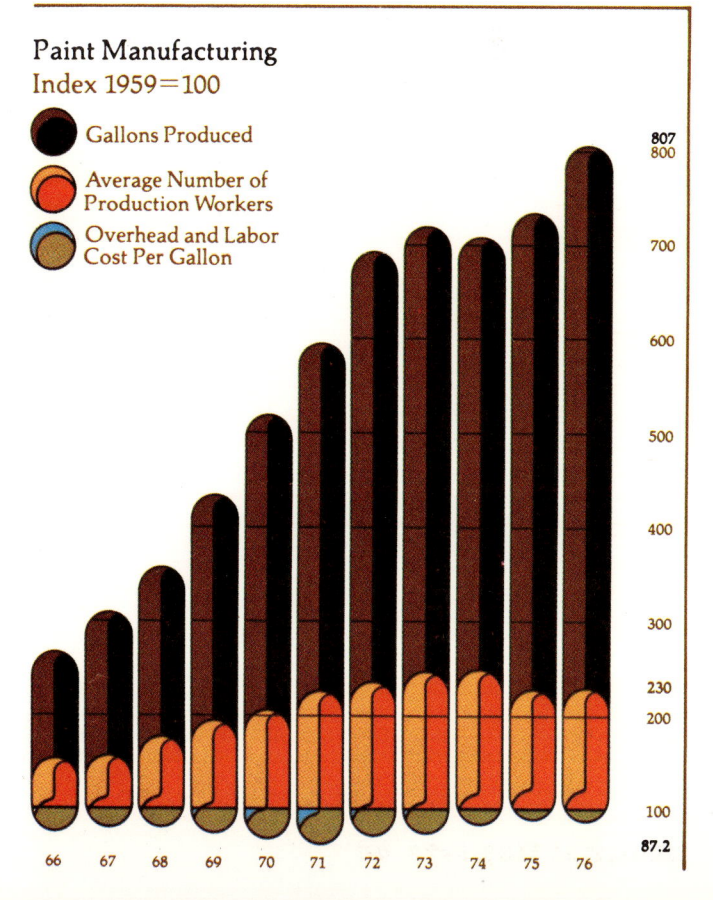

Paint Manufacturing
Index 1959=100

- Gallons Produced
- Average Number of Production Workers
- Overhead and Labor Cost Per Gallon

87.2

St. Regis

Cook & Shanosky is a design partnership devoted to the good idea clearly communicated. In this, its first report for St. Regis, the duo has used this philosophy to bring a diversified, forest-based company's report out of the realm of the ordinary to an enviable position as one of the two annual reports voted unanimously into this Casebook.

Actually, the design stages of this report took more legwork than one might imagine. Cook and Shanosky were sent around the country to various St. Regis installations to view operations and get a feel for the company. Working with financial communications advisor Bruce McGhie of McGhie Associates, who represented client interests, the designers conceived a visual format that would enforce a verbal theme throughout—St. Regis' broad-based printing capability.

By following a two-track approach (one for visuals and captions, one for business review), this report transcends "good taste" to achieve an easy elegance. The visual track—a left-hand page comprised of a full-color, varnished bleed photograph with its caption at the top of the facing page—functions as a complete information unit. But instead of picturing the people and places that make up the company, the photos focus on St. Regis' printing-related products.

The photos themselves are skillfully designed, dramatically lit still-lifes that impress upon the viewer the importance of printed words—not just as "the prime conveyors and repositories of human knowledge and historical data," as the report's opening statement reminds, but as the essential communicators of practical, everyday life. "What would it be like without telephone books?" we are asked. "Think of a supermarket filled with unlabeled packages." And so, Pygmalion-like, the wrappers for a carton of frozen peas are transformed through the camera into a convincing part of an elegant table setting; a precisely curled check-out tape atop a stack of kraft grocery bags has the impact of a sculpture atop a pedestal.

The tabular/text track of the design approach makes no less of its mundane fare. Usually serving as merely a foil for snappy visuals, in the St. Regis report this material becomes an integral component of the design structure. Occupying the bulk of the right-hand page below the picture caption, this text—a *fait accompli* by the time the designers were called in—describes, block by block, the achievements of each of St. Regis' capabilities or divisions. Typography here—as in the photo captions—is Plantin, a face with both legibility and character and which Casebook jurors termed "refreshing" in the sea of Helvetica enveloping annual reports.

The copy blocks are separated by hairline rules. The rules extend into the report's broad margin, where they widen and ascend until they reach the trimline. This is a subtle visual indicator of the firm's overall 15 per cent increase in sales (although

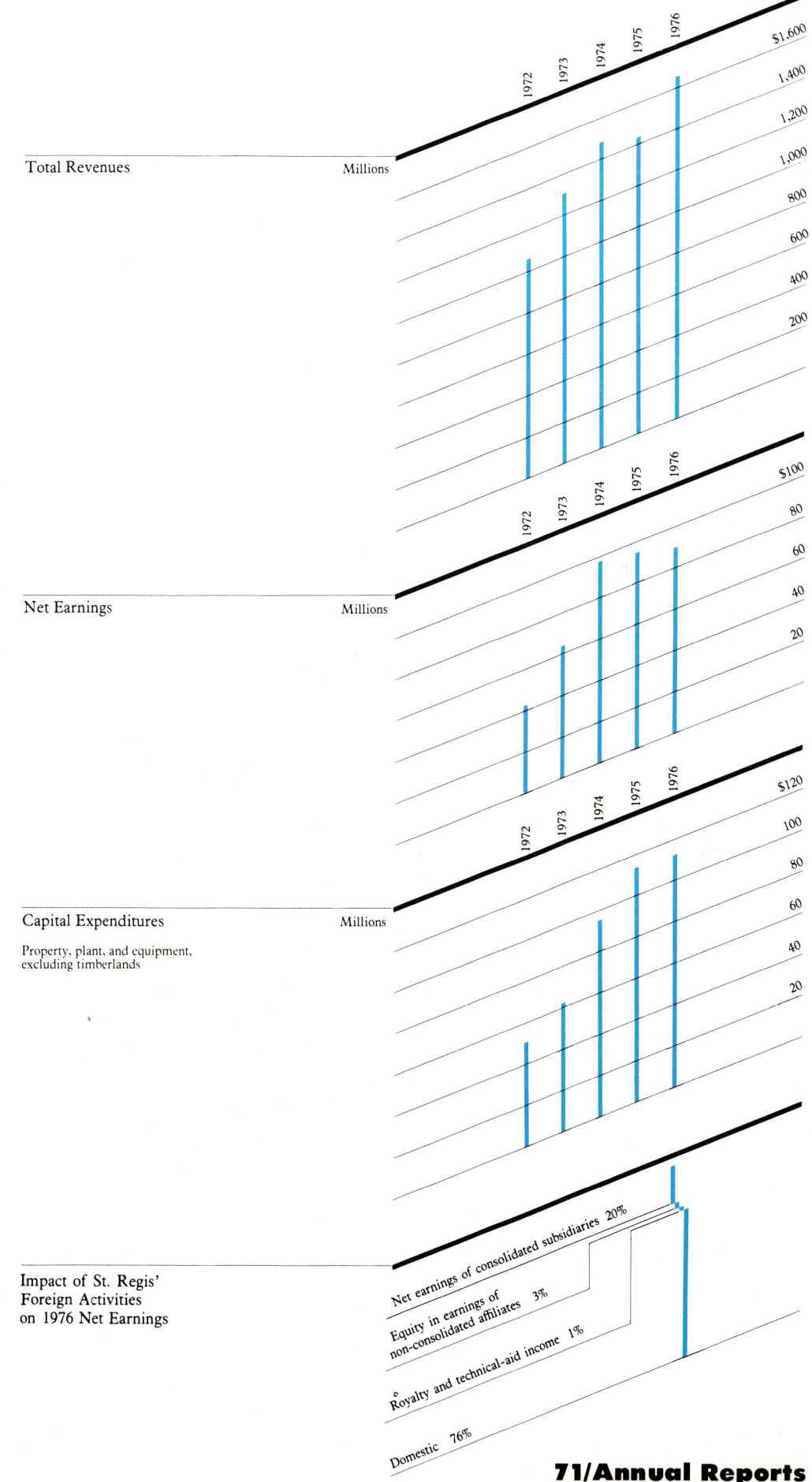

Total Revenues   Millions

Net Earnings   Millions

Capital Expenditures   Millions
Property, plant, and equipment, excluding timberlands

Impact of St. Regis' Foreign Activities on 1976 Net Earnings

71/Annual Reports

earnings per share were down by 11) and a device that makes tabular material both accessible and inviting.

The second half of this 36-page report contains the financial tables and the management analysis summary of operations. The charts in this section take two forms. The ascending rules prefigured in the first half of the report appear again to describe total revenues, net earnings, and capital expenditures. The remaining large tables—the straightforward statements of earnings, balance sheets, and similar financial data—are designed horizontally so as to be compatible with previous tables; hairline rules are used to separate categories and totals, and dollar figures are carried to their full three-zero representation. Here again, what the jurors considered an "elegant" touch—individual items within the broader categories are also separated by rules, but these rules are printed in a varnish that fairly shimmers off the page.

An annual report aimed at stressing the printing capabilities and involvements of a large paper producer/ packaging converter can be a tough assignment. Fine papers, good design and three days of overseeing printing have not only produced a beauty of a report, but have won the designers the opportunity to design St. Regis' next annual report.

Staged photos and an unusual approach to charts and tables make this report a unanimous Casebook winner.

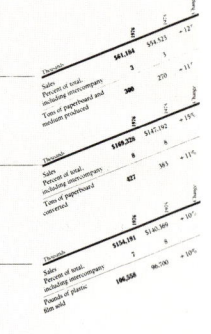

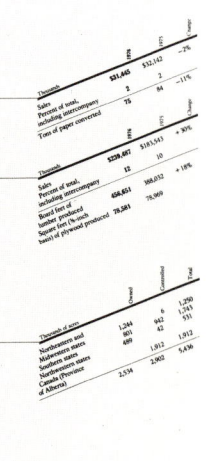

Report: St. Regis Paper Company 1976. Pulp, paper and paperboard; packaging supplying and converting; construction products; gas and oil. 1976 sales $1.64 billion.
Design firm: Cook & Shanosky, Princeton, NJ
Art directors/designers: Roger Cook, Don Shanosky
Photographer: Arthur Beck
Copywriter: McGhie Associates
Printer: Lebanon Valley Offset
Size: 8½" by 11"; 36 pages plus covers
Quantity: 110,000

Annual Reports/72

Owens-Illinois

This report proves that a client can make radical changes in a report's content after the design process has begun and, with the support of the designer, still achieve a masterly design.

As originally envisioned by Danne & Blackburn, the report for Owens-Illinois was to include a traditional narrative and a theme-based photo essay, printed in full color on enamel white stock. Financial reviews were to be highlighted with smaller, product still-life spots. After this solution was submitted, O-I management decided to include in the report three texty letters, one from the chairman and one from each of the firm's two presidents (one president for domestic operations, the other for international). The reason for the additions was a recent corporate restructuring which, it was felt, the report ought to reflect.

For the designers, it meant a trip back to the drawing board. There were new problems of organization to be contended with, specifically, how to include those letters without drowning the design in a sea of gray. The challenge was heightened by a feeling among management personnel that, because of various priorities within the operating divisions, no one overriding theme ("end-use," "manufacture," etc.) should be used. In addition, the book was to be produced at the same budget—$1.28 per copy—as in the previous year.

Danne & Blackburn's final solution represents an unusual design for this client—and for

Owens-Illinois: the Packaging, Consumer, Scientific, International Company. Annual Report 1976

O-I

73/Annual Reports

an annual report generally. Photos and text are separated into two distinct sections, with a separate paper stock for each. A format has been devised to utilize each page to its utmost (even the insides of covers cannot be distinguished from their neighboring pages), yet, because of a sensitive approach to scaling of copy and placement of rules, the report manages to incorporate a hefty amount of material without sacrificing clarity and legibility.

The report opens with a 32-page all-text form of tan, textured stock, printed in black and brown; this form wraps around a smaller form of velvet-finished white stock which comprises the photo section. The three texty letters have been greatly relieved by setting them in an up-size Palatino in broad columns that run one to a page. A second color—a rich sienna brown—is used for heads and rules and also to call out the quotes which hang from rules in the wide margins to the left of the columns. Each letter-writer gets an ample-size photo at the start of his message.

These letters fill the first 13 pages of this section; the last three—designed in the same color-ruled format—spell out Owens-Illinois products and facilities and list directors and managers.

The photo section in the center of the report is not a theme essay but a judiciously edited pictorial representation of each division's activities through one symbolic photograph. There are the computer screens used in package design; lightweight plastic bottles coming off the

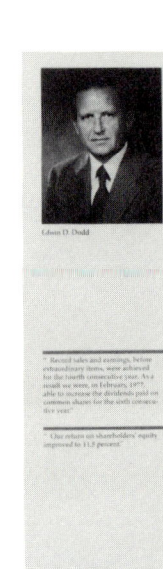

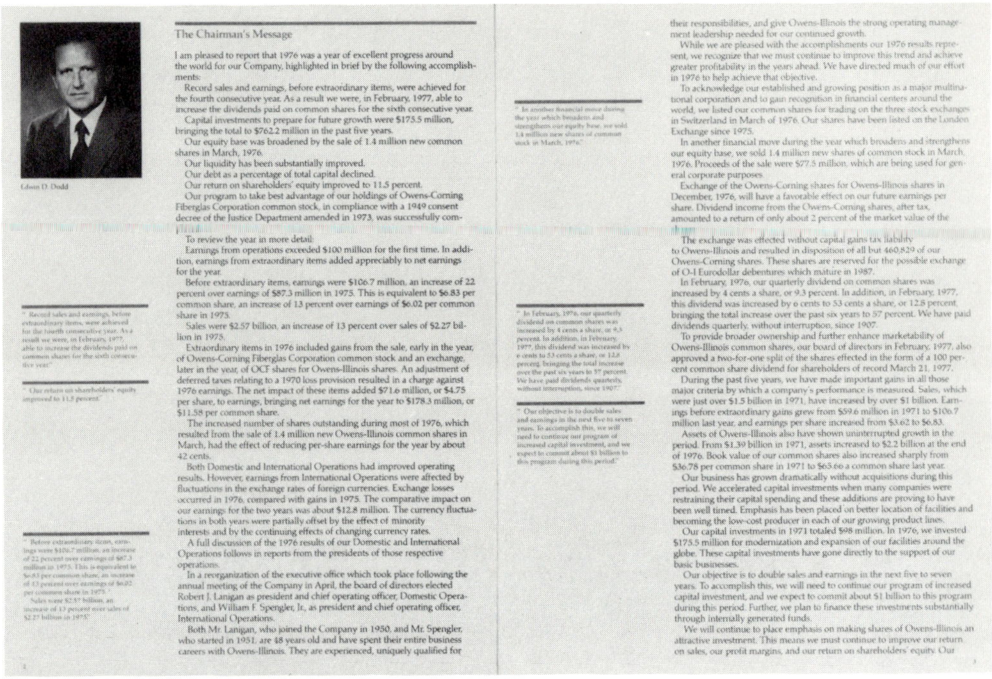

This report's deft organization of a lengthy text and judicious editing of photography represent design-as-problem-solving at its best.

Annual Reports/74

line; sparkling household glassware; the glass vials and syringes used in the pharmaceutical field. The pictures are crisp and clear and colorful, set up in a module that runs one photo full-page left, and a smaller photo lower-center right.

But typography is important in this section, too. The opening page bears no photo at all—just the words "Owens-Illinois: the Packaging, Consumer, Scientific, International Company at work," set in 54-point Palatino. (This is the same message heralded on the report's cover, with the words "Annual Report 1976" replacing the last phrase.) On the picture pages, large-type captions, printed in the rich, rusty brown used elsewhere in the report, vie for attention.

The photo section ends as it began, with a photo-less page bearing one printed message. Here, it is a ten-line paragraph promising increased profits and continued leadership in O-I's specific area of operations. The reader is now prepared for the remainder of the report—a return to the staid text-and-rules format that marked the opening pages. Here is the second half of that wrap-around, organized without fanfare into the text and tables that form the financial review.

Although extensive changes and combinations of papers and colors might be expected to increase production costs, this report was still produced within budget. The print run was designed as three 16-page web forms, plus one four-page form, sheet-fed, for the cover. Because of this care in planning—and because of the designers' dexterity in solving problems of content—the client got a report that looks much more expensive than it actually is.

Danne & Blackburn have three annual reports in this Casebook; they have also been represented in each of the previous editions. It is worth noting that, while other winning reports have followed a perhaps more predictable path to their excellent solutions, this report is a departure that represents problem-solving at its best.

Report: Owens-Illinois 1976. Paper, glass and plastic packaging and containers; specialized glass products; plywood and dimensional lumber. 1976 sales $2.57 billion.
Design firm: Danne & Blackburn, New York
Art director/designer: Bruce Blackburn
Photographers: Cheryl Rossum (most photography); ICOM, Inc. (page 24); John Fong (page 28); Heini Schneebli (page 30)
Copywriter: Owens-Illinois
Printer: Herbick and Held
Size: 8½" by 11¼"; 48 pages plus covers
Quantity: 85,000

75/Annual Reports

United California Bank

Several annual reports submitted for this Casebook responded in theme to the celebration of the nation's Bicentennial. Some of the books used patriotic pictorials —photographs of "Operation Sail" or national landmarks. But others took the opportunity to reflect on the current political and economic climate of a nation founded in democracy and free enterprise 200 years ago.

The United California Bank is one of these corporations, and its report is a combination of words and photographs that makes an eloquent case for the preservation of the capitalist system.

At the heart of the report is a thoughtful essay, "Capitalism in America's Third Century." While some such essays bandy anger and rhetoric, this one seeks a balance between the government's protection of the consumer, on the one hand, and corporate responsibility, on the other. It points out various failings in government-operated enterprises, such as the Postal Corporation; the various fruits of American free enterprise, not the least of which is the highest standard of living in the world; and the basic duty of business to police itself, or, in the words of Thomas A. Murphy, chairman of General Motors, as he is quoted in this report, to "strive for greater product quality and improved service" and to "admit when we are wrong—and correct our mistakes, promptly and fully."

Unlike many annual reports, where copy is almost incidental to an overall visual treatment, this report has been designed to provide a

Annual Reports/76

complementary environment for the carefully written essay. The report's covers are black —inside and out—with four small photographs grouped in the center front and back. Miniature versions of full-page photos used inside, these have been duotone-printed and spot-varnished for maximum definition of both subject and photo frame.

The report's opening pages present the financial summary and letter to shareholders in a restrained, ruled format in keeping with both the verbal and the visual tone of the essay to come. Printed on coated white stock, these pages are highlighted by two-toned gray charts that sit like miniature landscapes below the running text; on the last page of this form, two differently drawn charts—one, a dot-and-dash indicator, the other, a straight bar graph— are also printed in grays.

Page 5 opens the essay section of the book with a page of buff-colored rag stock that is bare except for the four-line title in the upper left. Set in a large reader face to one broad column per page, the essay continues for six pages and is interspersed with varnished, duotone black-and-white photographs printed on coated stock. The photos are dramatically-lit portraits of some of the people who are helped with money from the United California Bank. The emphasis here is not on indirect beneficiaries, but on the small-businessperson—a vintner, a flying-service pilot, a garment manufacturer. A few larger entities are represented—a hospital, for instance, and a publicly-owned

77/**Annual Reports**

sugar mill in Mexico—but what we primarily get a feeling of is a trust for people, just as the essay gives us a feeling of trust for the people who run America's businesses.

Following the essay is the organization review. The design scheme here follows that established in the front of the book: buff stock with serif type set below a continuing two-point rule. Type here is in two columns, although in the financial tables and notes it returns to the width used for the essay or goes full across the page. Four more photographs are included in this section, continuing the idea of people into the bank's business report.

This is another of four reports designed by the James Cross Design Office appearing in this edition of the Annual Report Casebook. Designer Emmett Morava writes that, in producing this report, he hoped to design "a very elegant, understated book in keeping with a carefully written essay on capitalism." "The visual impression is that of a bank," he adds; "businesslike, understated, conservative." This report has given him, and the reader, more than he hoped for.

Report: United California Bank 1976. 1976 operating income $385 million.
Design firm: James Cross Design Office, Los Angeles
Art director: James Cross
Designer: Emmett Morava
Photographer: Scott Slobodian
Copywriter: Larry Pearson
Printer: Anderson Lithograph
Size: 8½" by 11"; 60 pages plus covers
Quantity: 20,000

Fine duotone printing of charts and photos and the use of rag and coated papers create an artful environment for this report's thoughtful essay on capitalism.

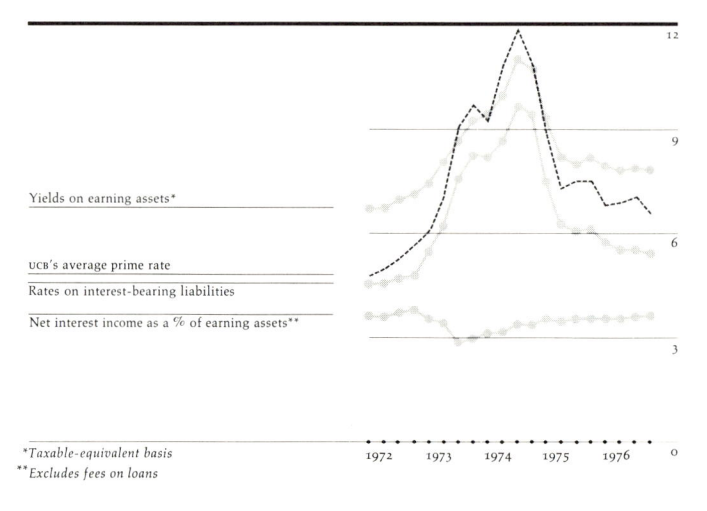

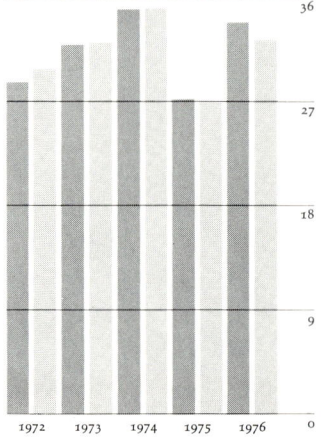

Annual Reports/78

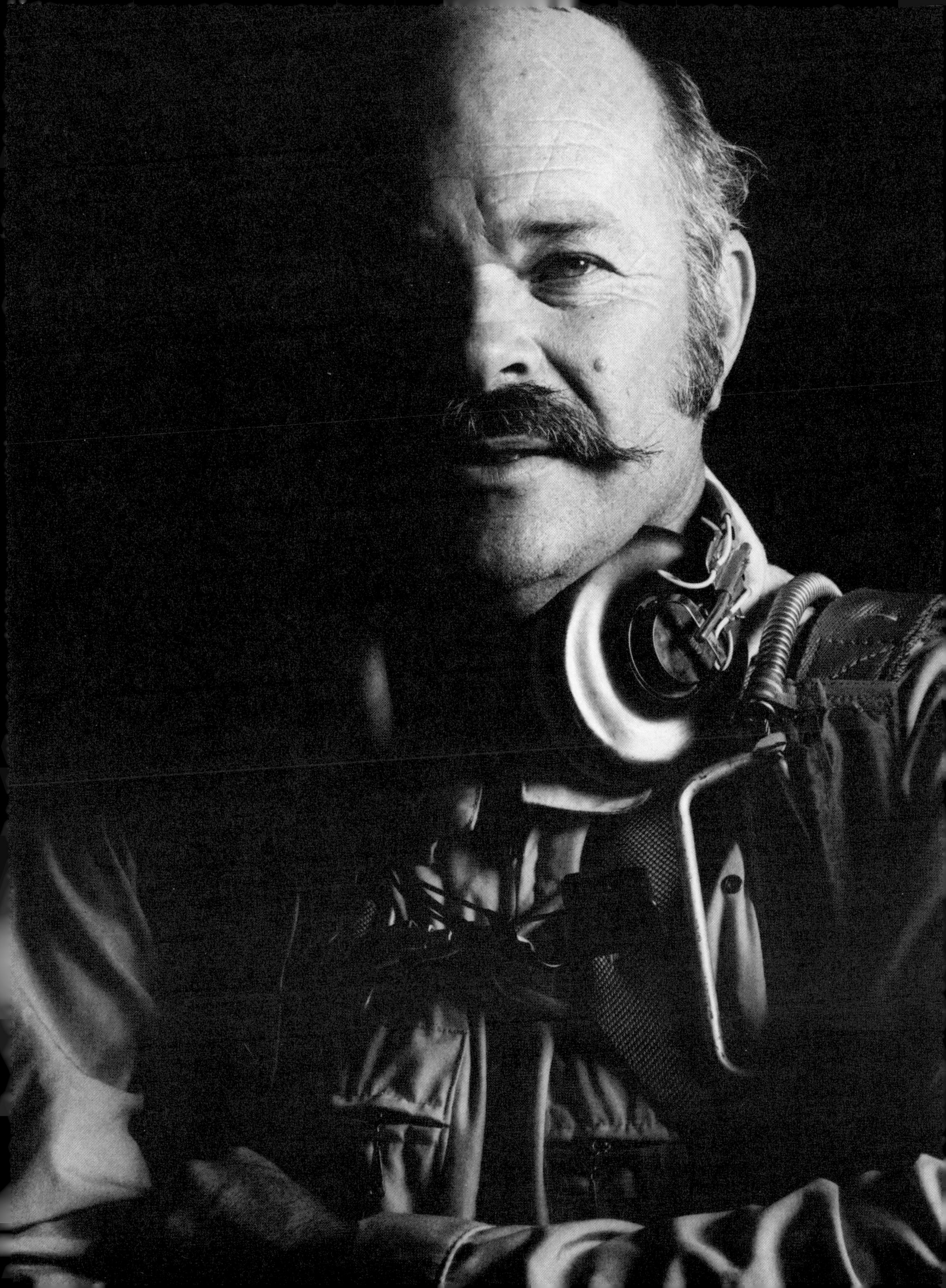

Lomas & Nettleton

Nineteen-seventy-six was another year in a series of bad years for people involved in the real estate business. Although the building industry experienced its biggest boom since 1973, particularly in the single-family market, financial institutions continued to be bogged down by foreclosures, bankruptcies, and delinquencies within the industry.

As in previous bad years, Lomas & Nettleton in its 1976 report seeks to create a spirit of optimism amidst the gloom. Featured in the second Casebook (this is L&N's third appearance in these pages), the 1975 report turned upon a theme of work and self-reliance. The following year's report turns first to the 1975 report, reiterating some of the positive thinking that appeared there: "...Some are so discouraged as to suggest that there will be no recovery; that indeed Chicken Little was right —the sky is falling. But, in our judgment at least, the sky is not falling..." To this, the 1976 report adds that, by mid-year, there were "some clear signals that economic recovery in fact had begun."

But the continuing source of strength for this company— and for the report at hand—is its apparent commitment to the land. The designers have sought to illustrate that commitment with sensitive landscape photography and quotes from American Indian writings. (In the '75 report, the visuals were about working people and the selections were from Walt Whitman.)

"The land, this earth around us, and the great natural resources that have given

LOMAS & NETTLETON MORTGAGE INVESTORS
1976 ANNUAL REPORT

"Here is what our Creator said: 'I shall establish the earth, on which the people will move about. The new people, too, will be taking their places on the earth. And there will be a relationship when they want to refer to the earth: they will always say, our mother, who supports our feet.' And it is true: we are using it every day and every night; we are moving about on the earth. And we are also obtaining from the earth the things that bring us happiness. And therefore let there be gratitude."

Annual Reports/80

"Wait here in the darkness!
Come, all you who listen.
Go the magic journey;
Now the sky is empty;
Of all sun and star-shine.
Come, we lose our footing.
Let us wait in darkness."

Lomas & Nettleton's commitment to
the land is portrayed with sensitive
landscape photography and quotes
from traditional American Indian
writings.

81/Annual Reports

America such abundance" is the theme set forth at the front of the report. By concentrating on the folklore and poetry of a "more 'primitive' culture," the designers hoped to give the reader "a perception of the land more basic than his own, thereby enhancing his appreciation."

And the writings are moving. The reverence of the Indians for nature and its rhythms, for harmony between the land and all the objects and creatures upon it, is based in a spirituality that speaks through their everyday life. Songs are sung to "blossoming corn," over which "wild bees hum." Rain is a divine act, sought in song and prayer. The land itself is moved and molded by an "Earth Magician."

It is a bit ironic, of course, that the beautifully photographed and lavishly printed black-and-white views of buttes and mesas and raging streams and peaceful fields represent the very land in which Lomas & Nettleton seeks to invest.

This report goes far in bringing to an essentially black-and-white exercise the impact of more expensive processes. The Dallas-based Richards Group has designed all seven of the reports issued by Lomas & Nettleton since its founding. Each has been trimmed to a comfortable 7" by 11" format; each has used photography and has been printed with a light hand, whether in black-and-white or in color.

The process used in printing the company's '76 report is Quatretone, a technique which adds depth and dimension to both black and gray areas of colorless photography. The photos were selected for their reproducibility in this process —all have good tonal range, with black-blacks and dramatic areas of white and gray.

There is no division of year in review from photography, except by spread: Photographs are framed across the double page every second spread, with the Indian writings appearing in Garamond Italic at the top. On the alternate spreads, review text is set in an oversize Garamond. Paper is an ultra-white stock with a dull-coated finish and an opacity well suited to the printing process.

Charts are handled simply, printed as horizontal bars in a gray pulled from the Quatretone. Tables are constructed with Garamond type and hairline rules on the pages near the end of the report. The whole effect is one of respect and reserve that works well with the soft mood of the visuals.

For the designers, this report brought the satisfaction of producing a black-and-white report (no money was budgeted for color photography or separations) that somehow achieves the drama usually reserved for more opulent, full-color productions. And for the reader, there are in the words and pictures some uplifting moments.

Report: Lomas & Nettleton Mortgage Investors 1976. Mortgages. 1976 revenues $22 million.
Design firm: The Richards Group, Dallas
Art directors: Stan Richards, Ron Sullivan
Designer: Ron Sullivan
Photographer: Greg Booth/ Francisco & Booth
Copywriter: The Richards Group; poetry anonymous
Printer: Heritage Press
Size: 7" by 11"; 40 pages plus covers
Quantity: 17,500

Annual Reports/82

"Over the blossoming corn,
Over the virgin corn,
Wild bees hum.
Over the blossoming beans,
Over the virgin beans,
Wild bees hum.

Over your field of growing corn,
All day shall hang the thundercloud.
Over your field of growing beans,
All day shall come the rousing rain."

83/Annual Reports

Amdahl

Amdahl is a new and fast-growing developer of large-scale computer systems for general applications. Founded in 1970, Amdahl saw its first revenues in the last quarter of 1975. Nineteen seventy-six was the company's first full year of operation, and at the end of that year, it had revenues (comprised of sales and equipment maintenance) of nearly $93 million.

This is Amdahl's first annual report, and it was important that it establish an image for the company, that it depict as clearly as possible what the company does and how well it does it. Obviously, Amdahl is a company that knows where it's going, and potential investors should get that impression from reading this report.

"There is usually a believability problem with new, high-technology companies," says Lawrence Bender, the designer of this report. For that reason, he chose a photographic theme to convey a "true picture of the company." The report is organized with text on one side of the spread, and a full-page duotone photo on the other.

Dropped into the black-and-white duotones are six small, square, four-color photographs that serve to amplify the larger — and often more abstract — shots of products and installations. This technique shouldn't work, but it does. The small pictures are arranged into an irregularly shaped module that is flopped in different directions from one photo page to the next, lending a feeling of activity and movement to the

Annual Reports/84

otherwise flat duotones.

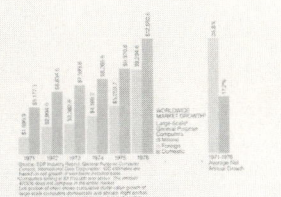

Text on these pages is also handled unconventionally. Although both running business review and captions are set in Palatino, italic is used for the running text while roman is used for captions (it's usually the other way around). The whole operations report thus seems like a whispered "aside," while photos and charts tell the real story of the company.

Actually, the charts were a prime consideration of management, who felt they could be used effectively to compare Amdahl's sales with those of "Fortune 500" companies. So, beneath the staggered columns of operations text there appears a single vertical bar graph, centered at the bottom of the page. Printed in the gray used in the photo-duotones, the charts compare expenditures, net income, return on sales, sales per employee, return on assets—all the areas where Amdahl is able to hold its own against that fabled "500."

Although the budget for this report was an ample $75,000, the designers were still conscious of ways to conserve capital. Use of some stock transparencies, for example, obviated sending a photographer to Europe, and the "Fortune 500" charts, which were originally to be printed in Amdahl's corporate red, were printed in the gray already being used for the duotones. Although this latter decision was made as much for style as economy, it did save the cost of running a sixth color inside the book.

The Amdahl red was used inside the report's covers,

Here, the designer experiments with the juxtaposition of black-and-white with color photography—a combination that shouldn't work, but does.

85/Annual Reports

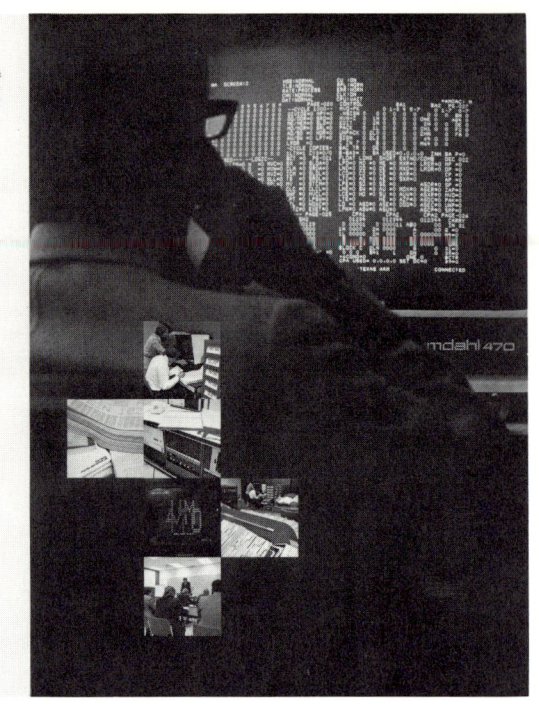

which are printed outside in a silvery metallic ink. The color serves to enhance both the monumental feeling of the report's oversize dimensions and the feeling of solidity and integrity established by its perfect-bound spine. Papers for text and covers are two weights of Quintessence with a dull finish that makes the most out of the gloss inks and matte varnish (over the four-color spots).

One other aspect of the design of this report deserves mention. The designer notes that the client's advertising agency account supervisor was part of the design team in the initial stages and helped to set the design goals for this report. In a field where egos abound and designers can be precious about their work being altered by an "advertising man," it's good to see that a spirit of cooperation and mutual respect can produce a good piece of annual report design.

Report: Amdahl Corporation 1976. Development, manufacture and marketing of large-scale computer systems. 1976 sales $92.9 million.
Design firm: Lawrence Bender & Associates, Palo Alto, CA
Art director: Lawrence Bender
Designers: Lawrence Bender, Mark Wallin
Photographer: Don Shapero
Copywriter: George Brown/ Lawrence & Lierle
Printer: Anderson Lithograph
Size: 9" by 12"; 30 pages plus covers
Quantity: 50,000

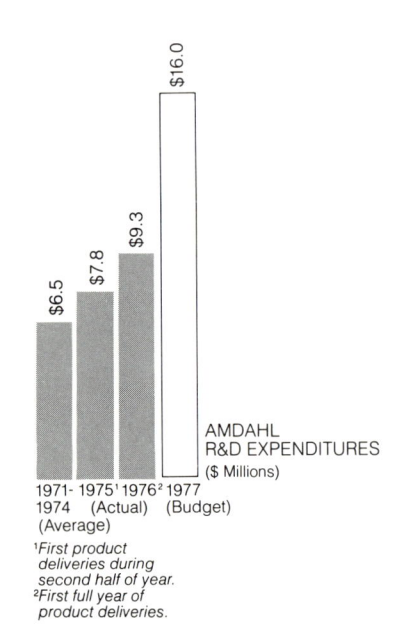

AMDAHL
R&D EXPENDITURES
($ Millions)

$6.5 — 1971-1974 (Average)
$7.8 — 1975[1] (Actual)
$9.3 — 1976
$16.0 — 1977[2] (Budget)

[1] First product deliveries during second half of year.
[2] First full year of product deliveries.

Annual Reports/86

Mattel

This is an unusual report for a toy company.

Mattel was considered a "hot stock" in the 1960s. A decline in the nation's birthrate, government and consumer pressure on toy makers' advertising and safety standards, and increased competition from within the industry seem to be the likely culprits for the company's slowdown; 1977 saw only a 13 per cent increase in sales, while net income and earnings per share were down.

Perhaps it is for these reasons that the 1977 Mattel report seems hardly in the image of a firm whose products include toys, hobby kits and films, a circus and a theme park. The designer notes that it was his intention to convey "a very business-like, efficient, non-decorated appearance" in producing this report.

One of the things that contributes to the serious tone set here is the extensive use of black. The inside front and back covers are lined with black, and black pages with reversed-out type serve as dividers for the two photo sections. Adding to the effect is a buff-colored rag stock that opens the book (providing a business-like background for contents, letter to shareholders, and company listings) and reappears in the back for the financial reviews.

Similarly, there is a good deal of restraint used in the handling of photographs in the two sections that follow the introductory pages. Here, photos are mostly full-color, but they are kept small. Pages are a slim 7" by 11" throughout the book; the

Annual Report to Shareholders for the year ended January 29, 1977

87/Annual Reports

business-review type is set in two columns, in three columns of captions only in the operations review. (These two reviews more often run concurrently in annual reports, and this two-section organization is a nice departure.)

Photos in the business review are barely larger than postage stamps, set randomly around the type; each shows a product or place or scene from a film produced by the company. In the operations review, a section filled only with pictures and captions, a few photos reach a rough 4" by 6". In responding to the questionnaire sent to Casebook winners, the designer gives no rationale for this highly modulated use of photography, other than "to make a less promotional presentation." One suspects that, because many of the toys themselves are gaudily colored and/or packaged, an attempt was made to keep at a minimum their intrusion into the businesslike design format. Here and there, a black-and-white shot helps maintain this atmosphere. The photos, the designer notes, "were done in process color and in duotone to give relief to what could have been a monotonous presentation." It is difficult to mix the two types of photography, but Casebook jurors felt they were successfully handled here.

As a design exercise, then, this report works. It has a well-organized visual presentation of both text and photography and plenty of white space. There is a nice hook-up between the white, embossed cover with its spot

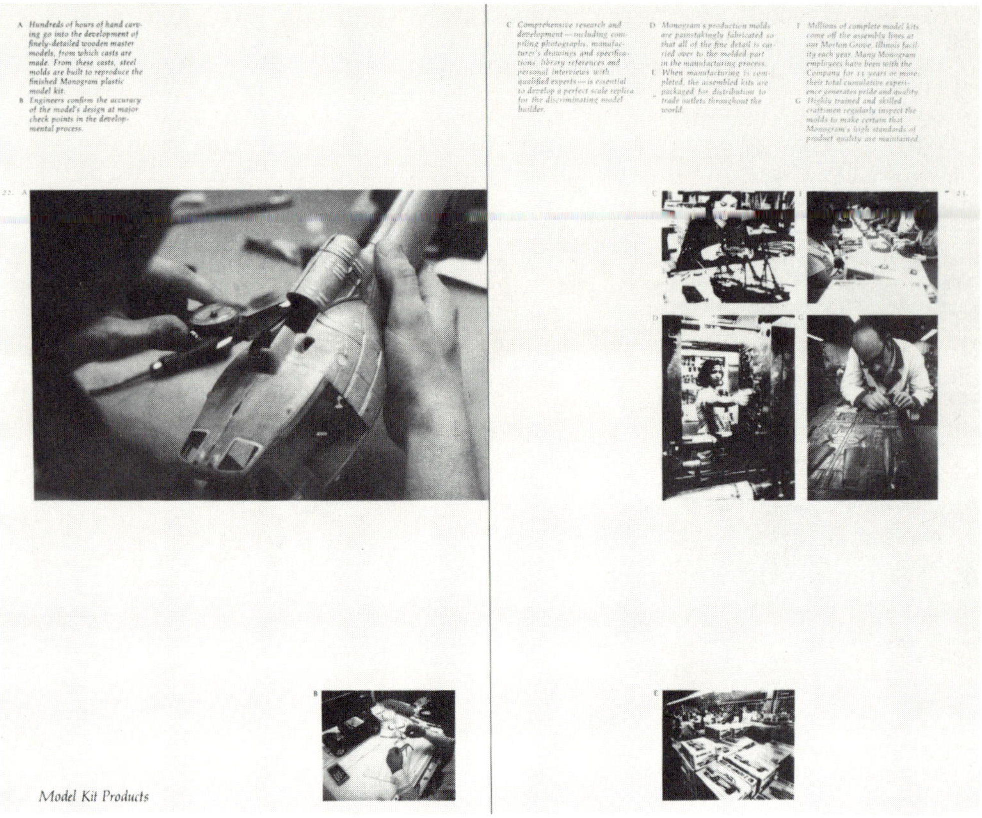

Model Kit Products

Toy Products

Annual Reports/88

photos and the spot treatment of photos inside. The use of rag text stock and organization of information in the financials does not want for clarity and readability. And the report is trimmed to a comfortable size. Though the reader might wish for more personality in terms of products, this report says that good fun and good entertainment can, indeed, be good business.

A restrained use of photography and a balance between text and white space says that Mattel is serious about marketing good, clean fun.

Report: Mattel, Inc. 1977. Toys, hobby kits, circus and theme park, films. 1977 sales $386 million.
Design firm: James Cross Design Office, Los Angeles
Art director: James Cross
Designer: Emmett Morava
Photographer: Scott Slobodian
Copywriter: Mattel
Printer: George Rice & Sons
Size: 7" by 11"; 52 pages plus covers
Quantity: 50,000

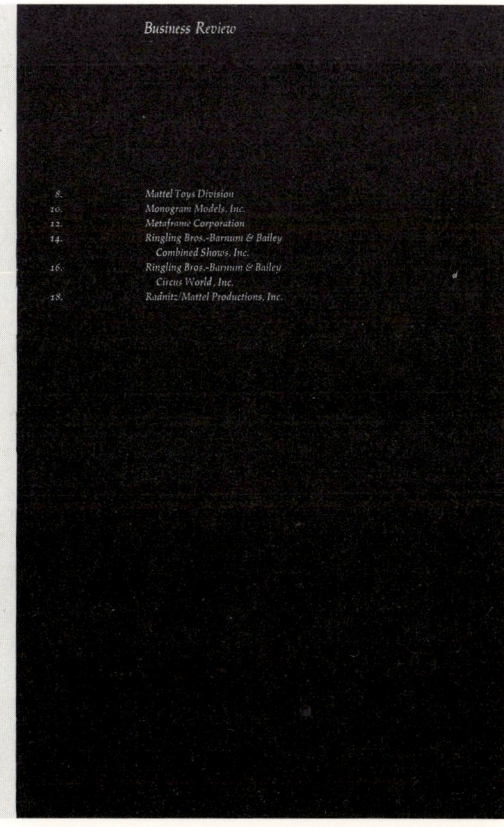

89/Annual Reports

Potlatch

This is the fourth annual report designed by Danne & Blackburn for Potlatch, and the third in a series of coordinated themes. The report continues the four-color, large-picture format established in the previous two; and—in an unusual bit of long-range planning—its basic design approach and theme, wood converting, were approved in 1975, when Danne & Blackburn produced the report for which this was envisioned as a direct companion piece.

While the 1975 report centered on the "more natural and esthetic subject" of tree farming, the 1976 report successfully wrestles with the problem of presenting a colorful and imaginative photo essay on what one might safely term a less exciting topic. Company operations and the people who run them may be standard fare for annual report pictorials, but photographer Burk Uzzle has managed to turn a pile of woodchips into a dramatic landscape and the production of paperboard packaging into a study in symmetry.

As Casebook juror John Morning observed in reviewing this report, "If you're going to gamble on a few photos shown large, those photos have got to be good." These are. As exercises in light and shadow, the full-color images heighten drama or create it where it is lacking. Even a dimly lit production line finds highlights on pipes and railings and density in a pipe-smoking foreman silhouetted in the control room.

Photo concepts, the designer tells us, were cleared before shooting by J.

Annual Reports/90

Alexander McGhie, of McGhie Associates, the financial communications consultants, and by Potlatch's president and chief executive officer, Richard B. Madden. Nothing like getting the OK right from the top.

An annual report has its public relations value, more so for a company whose business includes fine papers for printing. The paper used here is Potlatch's own Northwest Quintessence, a premium grade which takes admirably to the four-color-plus-varnish photographs which serve as the focal point for the operations review. Photos run double-truck, covering the lower three-fourths of each spread—or four-corner bleed for the first and last shots in this section. Captions, set in Garamond, are dropped out from upper- or lower-left-hand corners.

The remaining quarter of each spread is a running review of operations, strung out in three-column format across the top. Where one divisional report ends, a handsomely simple table appears to introduce and report earnings of the next division. "Potlatch is a progressive, well-managed company," says designer Dick Danne. "We developed the format to have a smooth, forward, horizontal flow." The typeface here is also Garamond ("It gives the report class and integrity"); heads are Univers, per the Potlatch CI style manual.

An interesting Potlatch practice is the inclusion of the company's ten-year record in the financial section of each report. And why not? The

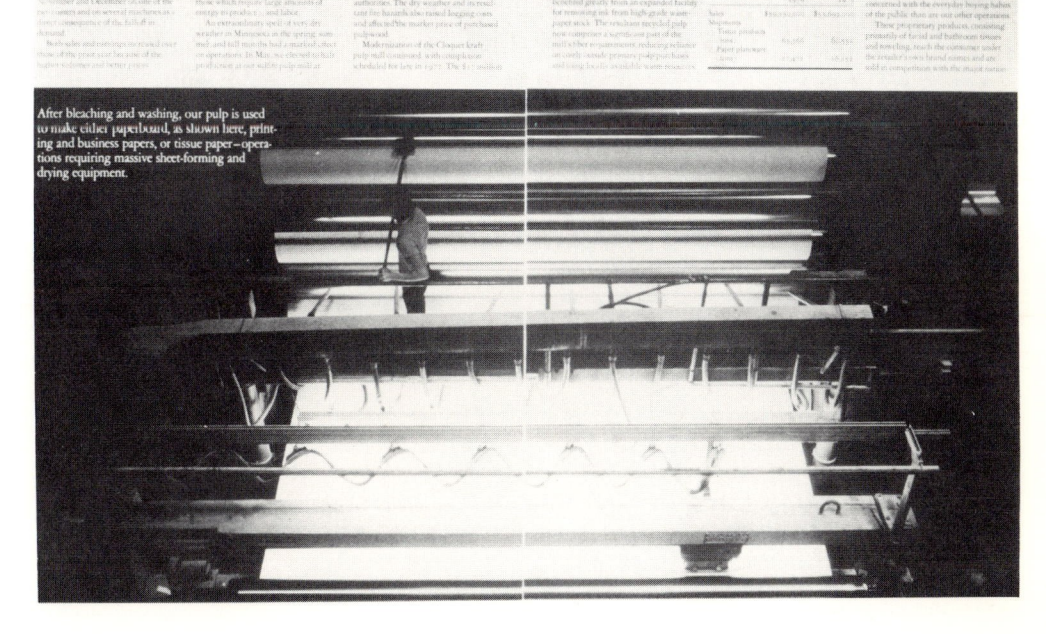

91/Annual Reports

company shows impressive growth over those years. The charts in this section are neat squares in colors echoing the chromes in the front of the book. The ten years are stacked vertically, so that the paper-white graph bars extend across the page, repeating the notion of horizontal flow.

The financial statements themselves have been organized into 30½-pica columns set off with rules reminiscent of the mini-charts that appear in the operations review. The columns appear one per page, leaving a 16½-pica white space to the left of each. Thus, the designers have relieved the hazard of gray matter in this section while nicely continuing the feel of the previous one.

One interesting anecdote reported by the designers has to do with the cover photograph—a wrap-around of snow-covered logs piled high and awaiting the trip to the mill. "For the first time in many, many years," notes Danne, "it did not snow in Idaho [where the photo was taken] until well into winter. We didn't get our cover until January 18."

Well, even the most skillful long-range planners couldn't have known that.

Annual Reports/92

Throughout all our diverse wood converting operations, Potlatch people are the element most essential to a successful manufacturing enterprise.

The third in a series of theme reports for Potlatch, this one handsomely depicts the company's involvement in wood converting.

Report: Potlatch Corporation 1976. Tree farmers and wood converters. 1976 sales $624 million.
Design firm: Danne & Blackburn, New York
Art directors: Richard Danne, Bruce Blackburn
Designer: Richard Danne
Photographer: Burk Uzzle
Copywriter: Alexander McGhie/McGhie Associates
Printer: Anderson Lithograph
Size: 8½" by 11"; 40 pages plus covers
Quantity: 75,000

93/Annual Reports

Colt Industries

The 1976 Colt report is the ninth designed by Arnold Saks for this client. It is an amalgam of the best features of contemporary annual report design, yet, because of some unique details, attains an individuality and cohesiveness that makes the designer feel that the Colt report is one of the most successful reports produced by his office in recent years.

More and more companies are going to a quick, at-a-glance profile statement inside the front cover, or on the front cover itself. In this report, that statement is set on the back of a vertical halfsheet opening the report (the front of this flyleaf is devoted to financial highlights). The flyleaf is a wraparound sheet from the pearl-gray rag stock used for the financial report at the back of the book. Interestingly, the two sections of the report—the coated stock operations review and the rag financials—are bound separately into the Lusterkote cover.

The flyleaf also features a pie-chart showing sales percentages for each of Colt's five lines of business. This is important, because that same chart appears—without percentage indicators—on the opening page of the review of operations for each division, with the piece of the pie in question dropped out to paper white.

Many reports use lavish, full-color photography. This report uses full-page bleed photos as dividers for the five business reviews, each of which opens on a left-hand page. Running vertically near the edge of the page is a

Annual Reports/94

9-pica-wide strip formed by dropped-out white rules. Inside the strip—again, dropped out to white—are the pie-chart and the division tag-line, set parallel with the rules so that the reader must turn the book—or his head—to see what section is at hand. Many designers would be hesitant to ask the reader to do this kind of fidgeting, but Saks obviously isn't afraid of getting the reader involved.

The photography—lavish indeed—focuses on the products produced by Colt—from valves and pumps and firearms to steel ingots, diesel engines and weighing instruments. All of the photos are run large—full- or nearly full-page, or spread across two pages. They are broken up by strips of the same dimension as those used to indicate section changes; these strips are used to hold nearly square photos of people who work in the various divisions, and to provide caption information about the large product shots.

While the product photographs are colorful and in some cases even spectacular, they are in no way mysterious. Their specificness is a welcome change from the dramatic but often unfathomable photography so often seen in reports issued by heavy-industry corporations. The designer notes that getting high-quality separations of these photos wasn't easy, but from the depth and range of the tones in the final printing, any extra effort would seem to have been worth it.

The financial section is a straightforward setting forth of facts and figures, organized

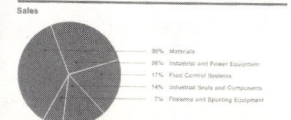

An amalgam of the best features of contemporary annual report design, the Colt report carves out its own identity with vertical identifying strips set into full-page bleed photos.

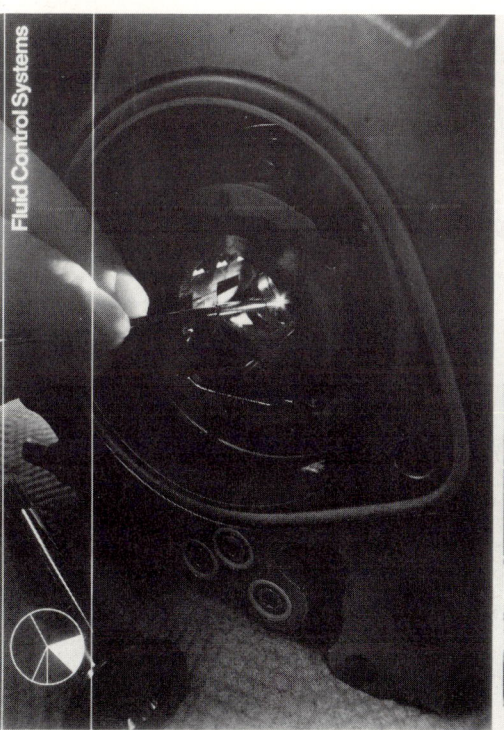

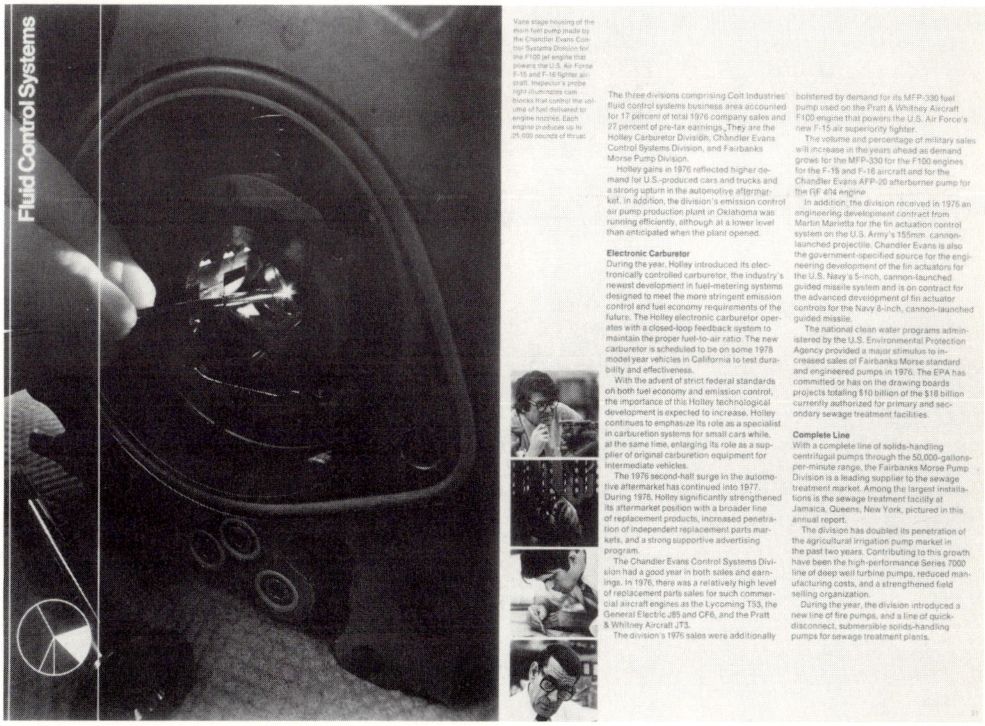

95/Annual Reports

with horizontal and, in one sales and earnings table, vertical rules. The six charts presented are simple vertical bars printed in blue over hairline dollar indicators. A useful "Directory of Operations" fills the last spread of this section, giving name, address and phone number for each Colt facility, along with a summary of the services performed there.

While repeat business from an annual report client is welcomed by any designer, Saks feels that the 1976 report is the "strongest visually" of any he has produced for this client, and would be hard to beat unless the editorial concept is dramatically changed. This is a problem many designers face—doing a good job and doing it differently for the same client year after year. It's reassuring that this designer, at least, can meet this challenge with some new ideas—and still maintain the continuing high standards he has set for his client.

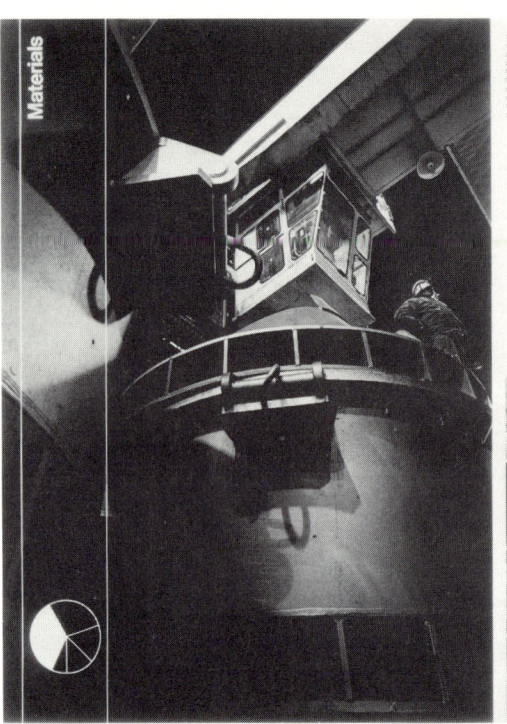

Report: Colt Industries, Inc. 1976. Diversified industrial products. 1976 sales $1.3 billion.
Design firm: Arnold Saks, Inc., New York
Art director: Arnold Saks
Designers: Ingo Scharrenbroich, Arnold Saks
Photographer: Burk Uzzle/Magnum
Copywriter: Colt Industries
Printer: Sanders Printing
Size: 8½" by 11½"; 48 pages plus covers
Quantity: 100,000

Annual Reports/96